COOKING

A Celebration of

EARTH'S GIFTS

School Sisters of Notre Dame

CELEBRATING
175 Years

Worldwide since 1833

International Standard Book Number: 978-0-9817090-0-0
(spiral bound edition)

Cover and book design by Gen Cassani, SSND
Cover photographs by Gen Cassani, SSND at the School Sisters
of Notre Dame Earth Spirituality Center, Mount Calvary, WI
Project coordinated by Linda Lynch and Patricia Stortz

To order or request information, please contact:
North American Major Area Coordinating Center
13105 Watertown Plank Road,
Elm Grove, WI USA 53122-2291
Phone 262-207-0047
www.ssnd.org

Printed by Murray Print Shop, St. Louis, MO, USA
using nontoxic soy and linseed based inks on recycled-content paper.

Contents

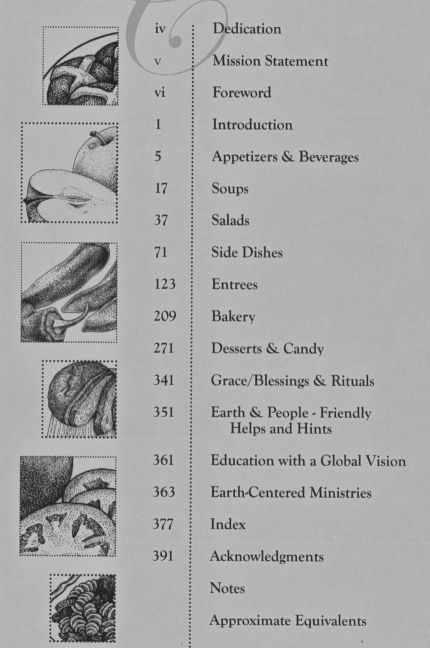

Dedication

to the
Mothers of our congregation

··

Mary, the Mother of Jesus,
Mother of the church and of the congregation
of the School Sisters of Notre Dame,

Blessed Mother Mary Theresa Gerhardinger,
who founded the School Sisters of Notre Dame,

Mother Mary Caroline Friess,
who led the congregation in its growth in North America.

At the end of each school day,
sisters blessed their students
and sent them home with these words:
"My dear children, I commend you to the Holy Spirit
through the powerful intercession of the Blessed Virgin Mary
and I entrust you forever into her blessed hands."

The Mission
of the
School Sisters of Notre Dame

....

Our mission is to proclaim the good news
as School Sisters of Notre Dame,
directing our entire lives toward that oneness
for which Jesus Christ was sent.

....

Urged by the love of Christ,
we choose to express our mission
through ministry directed toward education.

We are educators in all that we are and do.

Constitution of the School Sisters of Notre Dame

Foreword

Dear Friends of the School Sisters of Notre Dame,

It is with jubilee in our hearts that we share this **175th Anniversary Cookbook** with you.

"Cookbook?" You may be asking. "I thought they were educators!" And you would be right. As you will see from the opening pages, this cookbook is truly an educational adventure — one that will nourish the bodies, minds, hearts and spirits of all who share in its delights.

We want to express publicly our gratitude to all those who brought this cookbook to life: our SSND North American Major Area (NAMA) Development Directors, the Cookbook Committee, the recipe testers and all the SSNDs and SSND Associates who supplied the recipes. We are grateful to them and proud of them for their creative way of presenting SSND vision and values for the 21st century.

In **The Origins of Our Congregation** we read: *The congregation of the School Sisters of Notre Dame came to life when God's call found an answer in the hearts of people strong in faith, farseeing in vision, and courageous in action. The congregation continues today in the mysterious interaction of divine call and human response.*

Though its roots lie deep in the past, the congregation traces its actual beginning to October 24, 1833, when Caroline Gerhardinger and two other women began a common religious life in Neunburg vorm Wald, Bavaria. Their action was inspired by an apostolic spirituality destined to shape their own lives and profoundly affect those of many others.

We are grateful, too, for you, the recipients of this cookbook, who have embraced the vision and values of our founders and allowed them to affect your lives. It is through your collaboration with us that SSNDs from our North American Major Area are currently continuing our ministry of education in six Canadian provinces, 33 US states, Guam, Yap, Japan, Ghana, Kenya, Nigeria, the Gambia, Sierra Leone, England, Italy, Switzerland, Sudan, and Nepal.

We have much to celebrate this jubilee year. Our joy is increased by sharing it with you. May you have jubilee in your hearts each time you adventure into this **175th Anniversary Cookbook.**

In Notre Dame and on behalf of the leadership in NAMA,

Debra Marie Sciano, SSND
Provincial Leader, Milwaukee Province
Chair of the NAMA Executive Committee

Introduction

This cookbook comes from the SSND heritage that has brought us to this present moment, the 175th anniversary of the School Sisters of Notre Dame. Good food requires careful preparation. A meal is a time of sharing and a celebration of Earth, not only a gathering of human persons at the table but of the larger Earth community. Finally, as food nourishes our bodies, it also strengthens our spirits to make choices for the life and good of the generous planet of which we are a part. This cookbook then is about SSND heritage, the celebration of Earth's gifts, and eating as a moral choice and a way into a sustainable future.

1

Heritage

When Blessed Mother Theresa Gerhardinger, foundress of the School Sisters of Notre Dame, was invited to establish a school, she always made two requests: a convent near the church and a small garden. She emphasized the garden as a place for recreation in the fresh air and as a source of food. She talked about the importance of planting fruit trees and raising vegetables. From the beginning, SSND was rooted in the earth. Blessed Theresa wished to strengthen her sisters for the task of teaching young women essential life skills, including cooking, so they could raise Christian families that were physically, intellectually, emotionally, and spiritually healthy.

For the past 175 years, sisters have adapted their ministries to meet the needs of their time and place. Beginning with the education of girls in elementary schools, orphanages, day nurseries, vocational schools, and kindergartens, they

eventually included the education of boys when they began ministries in the United States and Canada. Today, School Sisters of Notre Dame educate wherever there is a need, always striving to empower women, to care for children and those who are impoverished, and to promote the integrity of creation, justice, and peace.

Celebration of Earth's Gifts

Sharing a meal, important in all cultures, is a central part of SSND life, fundamental for building community. Our Christian tradition has always reverenced the gifts of Earth: grapes and wheat, water and soil, bread and wine.

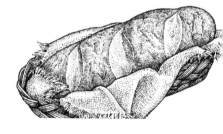

Coming together for a meal, we remember all the creatures, as well as sun, rain, and Earth, who generously contribute to the gifts on the table. We attempt to receive with gratitude rather than take for granted. Every shared meal extends Eucharist beyond the church to the table and finally to the entire community of life, from a human gathering to communion with all our kin on Earth.

Moral Choices: The Way Forward

As we enjoy with gratitude the bounty of the table, we also reflect on the interdependence of the entire web of life and the importance of a healthy planet. Because we interact with the rest of the Earth community through our food choices, eating is a re-lational and moral issue which calls us to consider the true cost of our daily bread: where our food comes from, how far it travels from its source to our table, and the impact of our purchases on the land, water, air, animals, and other humans.

Eating in a way that respects creation means acting just-ly for small farmers, for farm workers, for animals used as food, for rivers and soil and forests. Our food choices fur-ther destroy or ul-timately enhance the health of the planet and the sa-cred community of life. Our food choices today matter more than ever before; eating sustainably means that our children, and the children of all species, will also have enough to nourish them.

We wish, therefore, to reverence the gifts from the Earth community, to receive them gratefully, and to use them consciously and carefully, so all inhabitants of the planet may share in the abundance.

School Sisters of Notre Dame strive to be part of the on-going mission to transform the world through education. As food transforms our bodies and spirits, we are called to transform our relationship with Earth. We respond to this call by caring for God's creation and by seeking justice for all members of the sacred Earth community.

Through this cookbook,

we invite you

to bless the Earth
that blesses us,

to respect the seasons of life and of Earth,

and to reverence the creatures

who contribute to the richness

of the entire web
of life.

APPETIZERS & BEVERAGES

5

Blessed Theresa writes:

"*Our aspirants were asked to write you on the first, but they are delaying until the New Year. Babette and Amalia are well; Wilhelmine, the good child, has a touch of fever, but the present climate does more than medicine for the Hungarian fever. She enjoys the Bavarian beer, and it is good for her. The three of them are getting along nicely.*"

December 28, 1859 (#3001)
Very Reverend Bishop of Temesvar

7

Blessed Theresa Gerhardinger 1797-1879

founded the Congregation of the School Sisters of Notre Dame in 1833 with two other women. They began a common religious life in Neunburg vorm Wald, Bavaria. In their vision, the renewal of society depended on the Christian family in which the mother, the first educator, had a key role. Thus they chose the Christian education of girls as the vital service their community would offer. Their first concern was for poor girls in small towns and villages.

Today, Mother Theresa's congregation is a world-wide community of apostolic women religious in mission. Mother Theresa wrote thousands of letters which we School Sisters treasure.

Artist: Bober Stanislaw

Bean Dip

Tip: I tend to cook the beans overnight in a crock pot on medium but if I cook them on the stove, I stay in the kitchen so I can check on them. Keeping the pot uncovered helps me to remember to check. The beans can burn if I forget about them. I use a heavy, Dutch oven. The secret is to use everything fresh.

1 package pinto beans
Salt, to taste
1 large whole bulb (or 2 small) garlic, crushed
1 small habinera pepper, including seeds
or **Tabasco or Frank's hot pepper sauce,** to taste

8

De-Gas Beans: Pour boiling water over pinto beans and let them sit, covered, for two hours. Then, pour off the water; and it gets rid of bean gas. Some color will be lost also.

Cook Beans: Use a heavy pot to cook the beans so they will not burn. Cover the beans with fresh water to ½ inch above the beans. Cook slowly until they are mushy and don't pour off any water; with water loss goes the flavor. Add water if needed. Allow two hours of cooking on the stove or about 6 hours in a crock pot on medium.

Season: Add salt to taste, a teaspoon, plus or minus. Add garlic, crushed. Use a garlic press if possible. Add fresh, very hot peppers. Habinera peppers are best. Use a small one with seeds,

(continued on next page)

Note: When handling hot peppers wear plastic gloves and avoid contact with eyes.

School Sisters of Notre Dame
Celebrating **175** *years*

or half of a large one. Taste for hotness. If you cannot find hot peppers, use Tabasco or Frank's hot pepper sauce to taste. Picante sauce doesn't get hot enough unless you use a lot of it, but that tends to water down the beans too much. It's better to underestimate the water. Check several times, and add water. If the beans are getting dry, some of the top half (thin liquid) of the picante sauce. If the beans are taking too long to soak up the water, use a slottted spoon to strain the liquid off the picante sauce and add to the bean mix.

When fully cooked, mix with an old-fashioned potato masher or electric mixer. My dip usually has a "bite" from the fresh garlic but is not very red. I actually cook by looks and taste!

Submitted by Carolyn Sur, SSND from Saint Mary-of-the-Woods, IN

Champagne Punch

Serves 50

2 bottles champagne
1 bottle 7-Up
1 (6-ounce) can pineapple juice, prepared
1 (6-ounce) can orange juice, prepared
1 (6-ounce) can lemonade, prepared

Mix ingredients in a large bowl. Freeze a ring of ice and float it in the punch. Strawberries can be added to float in the punch as well.

10

Submitted by Susan Renner, SSND from St. Louis, MO

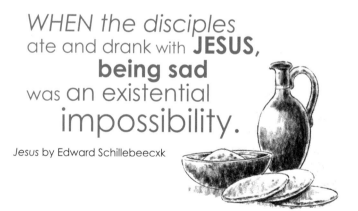

WHEN *the disciples*
ate and drank with **JESUS,**
being sad
was an existential
impossibility.

Jesus by Edward Schillebeecxk

School Sisters of Notre Dame
Celebrating **175** *years*

Festive Cranberry Punch

Serves 15

1 (64-ounce) bottle cranberry-juice cocktail, chilled
1 cup orange juice, chilled
2 cups lemon-lime soda or club soda, chilled
Orange and lime slices

Combine juices in large punch bowl. Stir in soda just before serving.
Garnish with fruit slices.

For a larger crowd:
Serves 66

11

4 (12-ounce) cans cranberry juice concentrate, frozen
12 cans water
3 cups orange juice
4 (12-ounce) cans lemon-lime soda

Submitted by Joan Frey, SSND from St. Louis, MO

Fresh Tomato Salsa

Serves 6-8

1 cup chopped tomato
¼ cup minced onion
1 clove garlic, minced
½ teaspoon hot pepper, minced
1 tablespoon lime juice
¼ teaspoon salt
2 tablespoons fresh cilantro, minced

Mix all ingredients together and serve with tortilla chips.

12

Submitted by Mary Beck, SSND from Mount Calvary, WI

Food is basic to life, and those who
provide it enable us to live.
Sharing food, the means
to life and livelihood, is what
a community does.
Breaking bread implies
that those of us who receive the food
pledge ourselves to justice for those who provide it.

Tomatoes

Sister Evelyn Mattern, "Hands of Harvest, Hearts of Justice"

**Learn more about the lives of migrant farm workers.
Are their wages fair? Are the immigration laws just?**

For information on the lives of farm workers: www.nfwm.org

School Sisters of Notre Dame
Celebrating **175** *years*

Hummus: Let Us Dip

Serves 4-6

This is a great recipe for snacking or even for a nutritious weekend supper and movie.

2-3 cloves garlic
1 (15-ounce) can garbanzo beans (chickpeas), drained and liquid reserved
2-3 tablespoons smooth natural peanut butter
A handful of fresh or dried parsley leaves
Lemon or lime, zested and juiced
Pinch black pepper, freshly ground
Pinch salt
2 tablespoons or less extra-virgin olive oil

13

Chop the garlic finely in a food processor. Add the beans and ½ of the reserved liquid and process finely or to a desired consistency. Add the peanut butter, parsley, lemon/lime zest and juice, black pepper and salt. Process until it forms a paste. Drizzle in the olive oil and process until it reaches the consistency of mayonnaise.

Serve as a dip with whole-wheat pita chips, carrot sticks, lettuce, celery, bell peppers, zucchini, or any raw vegetables.

Submitted by Christine Garcia, SSND from San Antonio, TX

School Sisters of Notre Dame
Celebrating **175** *years*

Mint Julep

1925
COOKBOOK

Serves 6

This recipe appeared in a cookbook put together by the 1901 class of the Academy of Our Lady (A.O.L.) in 1925 to raise money for the chapel.

¾ cup sugar
1 cup water
1 pint ginger ale
Juice of 3 lemons
4 sprigs of mint

14

Boil sugar and water ten minutes, and cool. Add ginger ale, strained lemon juice and bruised mint leaves. Half fill glasses with crushed ice, and julep, and garnish with a sprig of mint.

Submitted by Regina Lynch Grace from the Class of 1901
of the Academy of Our Lady (A.O.L.) in Chicago, IL

Love
all the **EARTH,**
every ray of God's light,
every grain of sand or blade of grass,
every living thing.
If you love the earth enough,
you will know the divine mystery.

Dostoevsky, *The Brothers Karamazov*

School Sisters of Notre Dame
Celebrating **175** *years*

Punch

Serves 50

1 (30-ounce) **Country Time lemonade mix**
4 (12-ounce) **cans lemonade**, frozen concentrate
2 (64-ounce) **cans pineapple juice**
103 ounces (12-13 cups) **ginger ale**

Mix first three ingredients and cool. Add ginger ale just before serving, using 2 parts punch to 1 part ginger ale.

Submitted by Nancy Traeger, SSND from Elm Grove, WI

 convent customs & traditions

School Sisters of Notre Dame observed customs and traditions which served to remind us of God's goodness and respect for creation.

"When I entered in 1962 in Mankato, Minnesota, we had wine on the Feast of St. John the Evangelist right after Christmas. I have continued the tradition."   Dorothy Zeller, SSND

ST. JOHN'S WINE - December 27

2 cups wine
2 whole cloves
2 cinnamon sticks
1 cardamom seed
¼ teaspoon nutmeg

Boil the spices in the wine for about 5 minutes. Strain the wine, serve hot.

Cooking for Christ, by Florence Berger 1996
National Catholic Rural Life Conference
www.ncrlc.com

School Sisters of Notre Dame
Celebrating **175** *years*

Southwest Eight-Layer Crab Dip

Serves 20

1 **(15-ounce) can black beans,** rinsed and drained well
1 **cup thick and chunky salsa**
1 **cup sour cream** (low-fat)
1 **(4-ounce) can green chilies,** diced
1 **package crab,** coarsely chopped
1 **small can black olives**, sliced, drained
1 **cup shredded cheddar cheese**
⅓ **cup green onions,** thinly sliced

16

In a 10-inch glass casserole, layer in the following order:

> **Beans**
> **Salsa**
> **Sour Cream**
> **Green Chilies**
> **Crab**
> **Olives**
> **Cheese**
> **Onions**

Refrigerate for approximately 30 minutes. Serve with tortilla chips.

Submitted by Nancy Traeger, SSND from Elm Grove, WI

SOUPS

from Mother Caroline's pen:

Owing to their real poverty, the parents could not pay tuition so we declared our first year among them free. To show their gratitude in the best way they could, they brought us the best and as much as they could from the fruit of the land and of their hard work: butter, milk, vegetables, berries, molasses, and a sweet juice prepared from fruits which brought a double blessing to our household.

19

The Letters of Mother Caroline Friess, School Sisters of Notre Dame, edited by Barbara Brumleve, SSND, p.30-31

Mother Caroline Friess 1824-1892

Mother Caroline Friess was one of five pioneer sisters to arrive in New York in 1847 with Blessed Theresa who was responding to calls for service in the new world. She was a dauntless traveler and wrote graphic and colorful descriptions of her journeys back and forth from the east coast to the mid-west, from north to south.

The SSND mission was enlarged in North America through Caroline's courageous leadership, her vision and willingness to risk innovative responses to the educational needs of women and persons who are poor.

Broccoli Cheese Soup

Serves 4-6

1 tablespoon butter or margarine
1 tablespoon onion, chopped
2 tablespoons all-purpose flour
1½ cups chicken stock
3 cups fresh broccoli, chopped
Salt, to taste
¼ teaspoon pepper
1½ cups milk
1½ cups cheddar cheese, grated
¼ teaspoon Tabasco sauce
2 tablespoons each fresh dill, parsley and chives, chopped

20

Melt butter in large saucepan or Dutch oven. Add onions and cook until tender, but not brown. Stir in flour and cook for 3 minutes. Whisk in stock and broccoli. Bring to a boil. Reduce heat and simmer 5 to 10 minutes. Puree the mixture in a food processor. Return to heat, and add salt, pepper, milk, cheese and Tabasco sauce. Heat thoroughly, but do not boil. Add dill, parsley and chives. Taste and adjust seasoning. Serve sprinkled with extra grated cheddar cheese.

Submitted by Trudy Csernyei, SSND Associate from Burlington, Ontario, Canada

Chicken Noodle Soup

Serves 8

2 chicken hind quarters, skinned
2 carrots, sliced thinly
1 medium onion, diced
1 cup celery, diced
4 cups water
3 teaspoons chicken bouillon
2 cups egg noodles, uncooked
2 cups hot water
⅛ teaspoon pepper
2 tablespoons parsley, snipped

21

Combine chicken, carrots, onions, celery, 4 cups water and chicken bouillon in a 4-quart microwave-safe mixing bowl. Cover with plastic wrap. Microwave 30 minutes on high or until chicken is tender. Remove chicken and allow to cool. Add noodles, 2 cups hot water and pepper to soup. Cover. Microwave on high about 12 minutes or until noodles are tender. Remove the chicken meat from the bones. Cut into pieces and add to soup. Microwave on high for 2 minutes. Garnish with parsley.

Submitted in 1992 by Joan Bartosh, SSND from Rochester, MN

Clam Chowder

Serves 4-6

5 slices bacon, diced
½ **cup onion**, chopped
1½ **cups raw potatoes**, diced
½ **cup celery**, diced
¼ **teaspoon celery salt**
½ **cup boiling water**
4 cups milk
2½ - 3 tablespoons flour
2 (7.5-ounce) cans minced clams, undrained

22   In large saucepan cook bacon until crisp. Add onion and sauté until tender. Add potatoes, celery, celery salt and water. Cover and simmer 10 minutes or until the potatoes are cooked. Combine milk and flour, stir into potato mixture and cook over medium heat stirring constantly until smooth and thickened mixture comes to a boil. Add undrained clams and heat through. Do not boil.

Submitted by Trudy Csernyei, SSND Associate from Burlington, Ontario, Canada

"**AND** you give them
their food
in due **SEASON.**" Ps. 145:15

School Sisters of **Notre Dame**
Celebrating **175** *years*

Corn Chowder

Serves 10-12

4-6 strips bacon, chopped
1 cup onions, chopped
1 cup celery, chopped
5 cups milk
1 (16-ounce) bag frozen corn
2 to 4 chicken bouillon cubes
1 teaspoon salt
½ teaspoon pepper
3 tablespoons cornstarch
¼ cup cold water

23

In a heavy-duty pot cook bacon thoroughly, but not until crispy.
Add onions and celery. Cook until tender, drain fat. Add milk,
corn, bouillon cubes, salt, and pepper. Simmer for 10 minutes.
Mix cornstarch and water. Add to mixture. Stir continually, until
chowder thickens and comes to a boil. Reduce heat and serve.

Submitted by Odile Poliquin, SSND from St. Louis, MO

Cracker Ball Soup

This recipe was served in the St. Louis Motherhouse every Sunday. It was lovingly referred to as "Sunday Soup."

Cracker Balls:

1½ cups powdered milk
1½ tablespoons baking powder
¾ quart cracker meal
8 eggs
1½ cups water
Chicken broth, enough for a soup

24

Combine milk powder, baking powder and cracker meal. Add eggs and water. Mix well and roll into small balls. Drop into boiling chicken broth. Let simmer until balls are double in size and fluffy. When dough is too stiff, balls will be hard; when too soft, they will fall apart.

Submitted in 1993 by Leocadia Meyer, SSND from St. Louis, MO (deceased)

Fish Chowder

Serves 4

2 large potatoes
8 or more fillets of small fish
¼ cup onion, diced
½ cup celery, diced
1 tablespoon butter
4 ounces cream cheese, softened
2 cups milk
Salt
Pepper

Peel potatoes and boil until almost done. Add fish to potatoes
and cook until fish turns white. Drain well and mash potatoes and
fish. In a skillet, sauté onions and celery in butter and then add
creamed cheese and milk. Mix well. Add to potatoes and fish.
Season to taste. Heat through but do not boil.

25

Submitted by Francette Malecha, SSND from Cambridge, MN

choose the right fish:

**The Monterey Bay Aquarium provides
a list of environmentally friendly fish choices.**

www.mbayaq.org/cr/seafoodwatch.asp

School Sisters of Notre Dame
Celebrating **175** *years*

Hearty Potato Soup

Serves 8-10

6 medium potatoes, peeled and sliced
2 carrots, diced
6 celery stalks, diced
2 quarts water
1 onion, chopped
6 tablespoons butter or margarine
6 tablespoons all-purpose flour
1 teaspoon salt
½ teaspoon pepper
1½ cups milk

26

In a large kettle, cook potatoes, carrots and celery in water until tender. Drain, reserving liquid and setting vegetables aside.
In the same kettle, sauté onion in margarine until soft. Stir in flour, salt and pepper. Gradually add milk, stirring constantly until thickened. Gently stir in cooked vegetables. Add 1 cup or more of reserved cooking liquid until soup is desired consistency.

Submitted by Joan Frey, SSND from St. Louis, MO

SLOW FOOD

In Italy, Carlo Petrini began **Slow Food,** a movement designed to resist the encroachment of fast food on the Mediterranean lifestyle.

School Sisters of Notre Dame
Celebrating **175** *years*

Heavenly Soup

This recipe appeared in the Notre Dame Centenary Cookbook put together by our wonderful "cook" Sisters in 1947.

Any kind of vegetable such as **peas, beans, carrots, and asparagus** which have been left over from a previous meal, to which is added some **celery** and **parsley leaves.** Cook together until tender. Strain through colander or sieve. Add a light cream sauce. It will make a nice Friday soup. **Potatoes** may also be used. Cubes of **buttered toast** may be added before serving.

Submitted by Mary Odilo Brinker, SSND from St. Louis, MO

27

Old-Fashioned Bean Soup

Serves 8

1 (16-ounce) bag navy beans
2 medium red potatoes
1 large onion, chopped
2 tablespoons butter or margarine
1 (14-ounce) can diced tomatoes

Soak beans overnight in just enough water to cover. Drain.
Cook beans in 2 quarts boiling water until soft (about 1 hour).
Add potatoes and cook until they soften (about another ½ hour).
While bean/potato mixture is cooking, sauté onion in margarine
until translucent. Add to bean/potato mixture. Add tomatoes
and simmer about 15 minutes until all is well mixed. Salt to taste.

Submitted by Paulette Zimmerman, SSND from St. Louis, MO

28

Potato Soup

Serves 6

2 tablespoons butter or margarine
⅓ cup celery, diced
⅓ cup onion, diced
4 cups potatoes, peeled and diced
3 cups chicken broth
2 cups milk
1½ teaspoons salt
¼ teaspoon pepper
Dash of paprika
Fresh parsley, chopped
¼ pound bacon, diced, fried and drained

29

In large pot, sauté celery and onion in margarine. Add potatoes and chicken broth. Bring to a boil and cook until potatoes are tender, 10-12 minutes. Mash potatoes with a potato masher until about half of the potatoes are mashed. Add milk, salt and pepper. Heat but do not allow it to boil. When serving soup, add a dash of paprika, chopped parsley and bacon on top of each bowl.

Variations:

For Potato-Cheese Soup, add **2 cups** shredded **cheddar cheese** when the milk is added. Allow cheese to melt. Chopped ham may be used in place of the bacon.

Submitted by Joan Bartosh, SSND from Rochester, MN

Pureed Cream of Cauliflower Soup

Serves 8

½ **cup onions,** diced
1¼ **cup butter**
2 **cups cauliflower,** cut up
4 **cups chicken stock**
1 **cup flour**
¼ **teaspoon nutmeg**
Salt and pepper to taste
2 **cups cream**

30

In a large pot, sauté onions in one-fourth of the butter until translucent. Add cauliflower and stock, bring to a boil.

Melt remaining butter in small saucepan and combine with flour. Add it to the boiling liquid in small amounts to thicken soup until desired consistency is reached.

Add nutmeg, salt and pepper to taste. Puree at low speed in blender. Stir in cream and serve.

Submitted by Mary Eric Militzer, SSND from Milwaukee, WI

Schwammnudeln

homemade noodles for soup

This recipe appeared in a cookbook put together by the 1901 class of the Academy of Our Lady (A.O.L.) in 1925 to raise money for the chapel.

Beat well **the whites of 3 eggs.** Into this pour slowly **the yellow of the eggs,** also well beaten. Stir same slowly with a spoon adding **3 teaspoons of flour and a little salt.** Then pour the entire mixture into your boiling soup, stirring the same with your skimmer. In a few minutes the batch is cooked. Take the noodles out and cut into smaller pieces for the soup to be served.

31

Submitted by M. Loyola Arnold, SSND from Elm Grove, WI (deceased)

The eyes of the Saint make all Beauty holy; the Hands of the Saint consecrate everything they touch.

Thomas Merton

School Sisters of Notre Dame
Celebrating **175** *years*

Sour Cream Soup (Kysela Vomacka)

Serves 6-8

A Czech recipe passed down for generations. This soup is even better the next day.

1 teaspoon of pickling spice
6 to 8 cups of broth
Salt and pepper
2 heads dill
1 onion, chopped
1 cup green beans, fresh or frozen
1 carrot, fresh, diced
1 potato, diced
Other vegetables as desired
1 cup sour cream
2 tablespoons flour
2 tablespoons vinegar
Small amount milk

32

Soup base / broth
Prepare your broth or soup base using any kind of meat: chicken, pork hocks, chicken gizzards, and yes, even beef heart cut into cubes. This is a great way to use up leftover chicken. Cover meat, including the bones, with water, bring to a boil and simmer for about two hours or longer. Drain off the broth, remove meat from bones and use in the soup. If you let the broth cool, you can skim off the fat before using for a soup.

Put pickling spice in a small cloth bag or closed tea ball and place with meat into the broth. Season with salt and pepper. Add 2 heads of dill. Add onion, green beans, carrot, potato and other vegetables and simmer until tender. To sour cream add flour, vinegar, and a small amount of milk to thin enough to mix well. Slowly add this mixture to the soup and heat well but do not boil.

Submitted by Francette Malecha, SSND from Cambridge, MN

Split Pea Soup

Serves 8

2 tablespoons olive oil
2 large onions, finely diced
3 garlic cloves, minced
2 teaspoons ground cumin
8 cups water
1 (16-ounce) package split green peas, rinsed and drained
2 bay leaves
3 carrots, finely diced
2 celery ribs, finely diced
2 tablespoons Tamari soy sauce
1 teaspoon basil
¼ teaspoon thyme

33

In a large stockpot, heat the olive oil. Sauté onions and garlic until tender. Stir in the cumin and cook about 2 minutes, stirring frequently. Add water, rinsed peas, and all remaining ingredients. Cover the pot and bring to a boil, watching for overflowing foam. Then reduce heat to a lively simmer, keeping pot partially covered and stirring occasionally, for about an hour or until soup has a fairly smooth consistency and vegetables are tender. You may need to add water as soup thickens. Salt and pepper to taste. For a thicker, heartier soup, add 2 diced potatoes and/or a cup of sliced mushrooms.

Submitted by Paulette Zimmerman, SSND from St. Louis, MO

Squash Soup

Serves 4

1 medium onion, chopped
1 tablespoon margarine
½ teaspoon curry
¼ teaspoon nutmeg
1 teaspoon Worcestershire sauce
1 tablespoon smooth peanut butter
4 cups chicken broth
4 cups squash or pumpkin, cooked
½ cup milk
Salt and pepper, to taste

34

Sauté onion in margarine. In a food processor or blender, puree onion, curry, nutmeg, Worcestershire sauce, peanut butter, 3 cups broth and squash until smooth. Put into saucepan. If using blender, do in two batches, adding to saucepan when pureed. Whisk in remaining broth and milk. Heat through but don't boil.

Submitted in 1993 by Regine Collins, SSND from Elm Grove, WI

Half of the 30,000 different items in the typical supermarket are produced by 10 multi-national food corporations.

Hope's Edge: The Next Diet for a Small Planet,
Frances and Anna Lappe

Squash

School Sisters *of* Notre Dame
Celebrating **175** *years*

Teddy's Potato Soup

Serves 8-10

8 medium potatoes, peeled and cubed
4 cups chicken broth
1 teaspoon salt
⅛ teaspoon pepper
⅓ cup butter or margarine
1 cup cream or half and half

Combine potatoes, chicken broth, salt and pepper in a large pot.
Bring to a boil, cover and simmer until potatoes are tender. Add
butter/margarine. Add cream and heat to near boiling, but do
not let it boil. Reduce to simmer and add dumplings.

35

Dumplings:
1 cup Bisquick
1 egg

Mix Bisquick and egg until well mixed. Using a spoon, drop
dumplings into the soup. Cover and simmer about 12 minutes.

Submitted in 1993 by Marie Torno, SSND from Chatawa MS

Vegetable Soup for Winter

···

Serves about 50

This recipe appeared in a cookbook put together by the 1901 class of the Academy of Our Lady (A.O.L.) in 1925 to raise money for the chapel.

½ **bushel ripe tomatoes**
½ **peck string beans**
8 large onions
3 bunches carrots
3 bunches celery
1 bunch parsley
1 bunch leeks
1 head cabbage
1 large sweet red pepper
½ **cup salt**

36

Chop or grind above vegetables before boiling. Combine all ingredients and boil In 3 gallons water for three hours. Fill glass jars and seal.

Submitted in 1993 by Mary Agnetis, SSND (deceased)

SALADS

37

Blessed Theresa writes:

To the Very Honorable Countess of Gorizia

"...What a wonderful surprise we had on receiving
your valuable gifts, natural products from your own
Illyrian soil. Please accept our deepest thanks. The
raisins of such excellent quality are a most unusual
gift for us in Bavaria. I was particularly glad that
they came just when our Reverend Inspector was
recuperating from a serious illness. The excellent
wine and the incomparable olive oil are no less
welcome."

Munich, March 16, 1859 (# 2854)

39

Beet Pickles

Serves 8-10

1¼ cups sugar
1 cup vinegar
1¼ cups cold water
1 tablespoon pickling spices, in a spice bag
8-10 small beets, cooked, peeled and sliced

Boil together first four ingredients for 3-5 minutes and let cool.
Place beets in bowl, add the syrup and cover. Refrigerate for
several days before serving. Will keep 4-6 weeks.

40   Submitted by Bernelle Taube, SSND from Northfield, MN

Gorgeous GARNET-COLORED *Beets*

Beets are loaded with antioxidants
which help prevent cancer. Fresh
beets have savory greens which
are not to be discarded.
They contain plenty of fiber,
potassium, beta-carotene and
vitamin K. They can be prepared
as you would Swiss chard. Just sauté
the chopped stems and leaves with
a little garlic.

BEETS have the highest sugar
content of any vegetable. A half cup of cooked beets
has only 37 calories. **HOW SWEET IT IS!**

School Sisters of Notre Dame
Celebrating **175** *years*

Broccoli Salad

Serves 4

1 bunch fresh broccoli, washed, broken into flowerets
1 pound bacon, fried crisp, drained and crumbled
½ red onion, chopped
1 cup celery, chopped
½ cup raisins

Combine salad ingredients.

Dressing:
¾ cup mayonnaise
¼ cup sugar
2 tablespoons vinegar

41

Mix thoroughly and pour over salad ingredients. Stir to blend.
Serve chilled.

Submitted by Sharon Rempe, SSND from St. Louis, MO

Carrot Salad

1947
COOKBOOK

Serves 6

This recipe appeared in the Notre Dame Centenary Cookbook put together by our wonderful "cook" Sisters in 1947.

3 cups raw carrots, ground
6 marshmallows, cut fine
½ **cup dates,** cut small
¼ **cup vinegar**
Sugar, to taste
½ **cup pineapple**
1 cup mayonnaise

42

Mix well and serve on a lettuce leaf or in a nice salad dish.

Submitted by Mary Venard, SSND from Lonsdale, MN as in 1947 book

Chunky Chicken Salad

Serves 3-4

2 cups chicken, cooked, diced
1 cup celery, diced
½ cup Grape Nuts cereal
½ cup mayonnaise
2 hard boiled eggs, chopped
¼ cup pickle relish
2 tablespoons lemon juice
1 teaspoon salt
Dash of pepper
Lettuce leaves, washed and dried
Cherry tomatoes (optional)
Carrot, peeled and made into curls (optional)

43

Combine all ingredients except lettuce, tomatoes and carrot curls. Mix lightly. Serve on lettuce leaves. If desired, garnish with cherry tomatoes and carrot curls. Sprinkle with additional cereal.

Submitted by Joan Bartosh, SSND from Rochester, MN

Cole Slaw Dressing

Serves 10-12

This is a tasty recipe that comes in handy when you don't have time to make dressing with each serving.

1 cup sugar
1 cup oil
½ cup vinegar
½ cup chopped onion
1 teaspoon dry ground mustard
2 teaspoons celery seed

44

Mix ingredients well. Store extra dressing in a jar in the refrigerator. It keeps a long time.

Submitted by Cheryl Marie Wagner, SSND from Mankato, MN

Cranberry-Pear Relish

Makes about 3¼ cups

1½ **cups sugar**
½ **cup water**
1 **(12-ounce) package cranberries** (3 cups)
2 **medium pears,** cored and cubed (2 cups)
½ **teaspoon nutmeg,** ground
½ **teaspoon allspice,** ground
Stick cinnamon

In a 2-quart saucepan bring sugar and water to boil, stirring to
dissolve sugar. Boil rapidly, uncovered, for 5 minutes.

45

Add cranberries, pears, nutmeg, allspice, and cinnamon. Return
to boil. Cook for 3-4 minutes or until cranberry skins pop, stirring
occasionally. Remove from heat. Cover and chill.
Remove cinnamon before serving.

Submitted by Joel Christy, SSND from Charleston, WV

Cucumbers

Makes 2 quarts

2 quarts cucumbers, peeled and sliced
1 large onion, sliced
2 tablespoons salt
½ cup white vinegar
½ cup sugar

In a large bowl, mix together cucumbers, onion and salt. Cover and refrigerate for 24 hours. Add vinegar and sugar. Stir well. Cover and refrigerate for 24 hours. Put in freezer containers and enjoy crisp cucumbers in winter. Thaw before serving.

46

Submitted by Bernita Wasinger, SSND from Jefferson City, MO

We cannot love God unless we love each other,
and to love each other we must know each other.

We know God in the breaking of bread, and
we know each other in the breaking of bread,
and we are not alone anymore.
Heaven is a banquet
and life is a banquet too,
even with a crust,
where there is companionship.

Dorothy Day, *The Long Loneliness*

School Sisters of Notre Dame
Celebrating **175** *years*

Exotic Salad with Tuna
···

Serves 8-10

½ **red pepper,** cut in thin slices
1 **lemon,** juiced and zested
Salt and pepper
⅓ **cup olive oil**
1 **mature avocado**
2 **large tomatoes**
1 **(10-ounce) can of tuna,** reserve the oil
1 **small head lettuce**
1 **small head escarole**
1 **teaspoon mustard or anchovy paste**

47

Grill or roast the red pepper in the oven. Grate the skin of half the lemon, putting the grating in a tureen together with several spoonfuls of lemon juice, adding a pinch of salt and a little pepper. Beat in the olive oil.

Cut the avocado in half, cutting around the big stone. (Use a stainless steel knife.) Cut off the skins always using the same sharpened knife; cut the pulp into cubes putting them immediately in the prepared lemon juice mixture. Wash the tomatoes well; dry; cut in half and remove the seeds; then, cut the tomatoes. Add to avocado mixture. Add tuna.

Peel apart the lettuce eliminating the tough parts; wash and drain. Place in a salad bowl. Pour in the tuna, avocado and tomatoes. Sprinkle with the slices of red pepper and a little ground pepper. Pour the oil from the tuna in a bowl. Mix in the

(continued on next page)

School Sisters of Notre Dame
Celebrating **175** *years*

remaining lemon zest and juice, salt, pepper and mustard or anchovy paste. Pour mixture over the contents in the salad bowl.

Submitted in 1991 by the Sisters of the Italian Province

English translation: Frances Ruggeri Stephens from St. Louis, MO

....

....

Health

GOD calls us to consider **what is "ENOUGH"** and to treat our bodies with RESPECT.

As rates of obesity and related diseases rise, North America's cheap, abundant food supply has become both a blessing and a curse.

Depending on how food is grown/raised, it can either damage or build up the health of the people and communities doing the growing.

Simply in Season Study Guide
www.worldcommunitycookbook.org/season/studyguide.html

Five Cup Salad

Serves 6-8

1 cup miniature marshmallows
1 cup mandarin oranges, drained
1 cup chunk pineapple, drained
1 cup sour cream
1 cup shredded coconut

Combine all ingredients. Chill at least one hour before serving, or for best results, chill overnight.

Submitted in 1993 by Marie Torno, SSND from Chatawa, MS

49

Fresh Green Salad with Lemon Honey Dressing

Serves 4-6

Lettuce of various kinds, bib, leaf, endive, torn in small pieces enough for four people
1 cup walnuts, chopped
1 cup dried figs, sliced
1 fennel bulb, sliced in small pieces
(Fennel is sometimes sold in grocery stores under the name Anise)
Blue cheese or other sharp cheese (optional)

Dressing:

½ **cup fresh lemon juice**
½ **cup honey**
¼ **cup olive oil**
1 teaspoon lemon zest (grate the rind of a lemon)

50

Mix and shake dressing. Put lettuce in large bowl, add dressing and toss. Sprinkle with walnuts, sliced figs, and sliced fennel. Add bleu cheese or any other sharp cheese of your choice. Mix again or leave it as is.

Submitted by Gen Cassani, SSND from St. Louis, MO

Know what you are eating:

read labels.

School Sisters of Notre Dame
Celebrating **175** *years*

Frozen Fruit Salad
···

Serves 8-10

12 large marshmallows, quartered
1 cup mayonnaise
1 cup whipping cream, whipped
½ cup cream cheese
½ cup maraschino cherries
2 cups canned fruit (pears, pineapple or peaches), cut in half,
reserve juice from canned fruit
Lettuce leaves

Combine marshmallows and fruit juice. Let stand until
marshmallows have softened. Combine mayonnaise, whipped   **51**
cream, and cheese. Mix until creamy, then add fruit and
marshmallows. Pour into refrigerator tray and freeze 3 hours. Cut
into squares and serve on lettuce leaf.

Submitted in 1993 by Mary Eric Militzer, SSND from Milwaukee, WI

Fruit Salad with Pretzels

Serves 12

½ **cup butter or margarine**
1 **cup sugar,** divided
1 **cup pretzels,** crushed
1 **(8-ounce) package cream cheese**
1 **(20-ounce) can crushed pineapple,** drained
1 **(8-ounce) container whipped topping,** thawed

Melt butter. Add ½ cup sugar and pretzels. Place on cookie sheet and bake at 400 degrees for 7 minutes. Remove from oven and cool slightly. While warm, mix and crumble into pea-size pieces. Set aside.

52

Soften cream cheese, mix in remaining sugar and blend well. Add drained pineapple. Fold in whipped topping and let stand. When ready to serve mix in pretzel crunch.

Submitted by Barbara Simek, SSND from Prior Lake, MN

Ginny's Cranberry Salad

Serves 8-10

1 (16-ounce) can whole berry cranberry sauce or 1 pound raw cranberries, chopped
1 (8-ounce) cream cheese
2 tablespoons sugar (¾ cup if raw cranberries are used)
2 tablespoons mayonnaise
1 (20-ounce) can crushed pineapple, drained
½ cup nuts, chopped
1 package Dream Whip, prepared

Pulse the cranberries in a food processor. In a bowl add cranberries to remaining ingredients until combined. Serve chilled.

53

Submitted by Ginny Draeger, Associate from Milwaukee, WI

Grow something edible even if it is only IN A FLOWER POT.

SIMPLY IN SEASON, a cookbook produced by the Mennonite Central Committee.

http://www.worldcommunitycookbook.org/season/index.html

School Sisters of Notre Dame
Celebrating **175** *years*

Grape Salad

Serves 8-10

1 (8-ounce) package cream cheese, softened
1 cup sour cream
1 teaspoon vanilla
4 individual packets of Splenda
2-3 pounds red seedless grapes, cut in half
1 cup pecans, chopped
½ cup brown sugar

Mix together the softened cream cheese, sour cream, vanilla and Splenda. Stir in grapes. Mix together the pecans and brown sugar, then stir into the grape mixture. Chill and enjoy.

54

Submitted by Sisters from St. Mary of the Pines, Chatawa, MS

Lime Butter Mint Jello Salad

Serves 10-15

1 (3-ounce) package lime jello
1 (13-ounce) can crushed pineapple, undrained
1 (10-ounce) bag miniature marshmallows
1 (8-ounce) carton whipped topping
1 (10-ounce) package butter mints, cut into pieces

Mix jello, pineapple and marshmallows. Stir well so jello dissolves.
Let stand covered in the refrigerator overnight. The next day add
the whipped topping and butter mints. Put in freezer. Will last a
long time.

55

Submitted by Marjorie Rosenau, SSND from St. Paul, MN

Mediterranean Mixed Salad

Serves 8-10

2 pounds very ripe tomatoes, remove excess juice
Salt and pepper
3 tablespoons olive oil
8 slices of bread
2 cloves garlic
1 pound baby (early) **onions**
2 yellow peppers
4-5-ounces black olives, drained, coarsely chopped
3 carrots, peeled and grated or cut into matchsticks
Parsley, chopped

56

Put a saucepan filled with water on the stove. Bring water to a boil and immerse the whole tomatoes, letting them boil for a minute. Drain them and peel as soon as possible. Cut them in thin rounds and distribute them in individual salad plates. Salt and pepper them; season them with a trickle of olive oil. Let them settle down for ten or so minutes.

Toast the bread slices in the oven; rub them with garlic; chop them into cubes; and keep them warm. Peel the onions; cut them into rings; and fry them in a pan until they are lightly brown. Skewer the whole peppers on a large fork, scorch them over a flame. Peel them, cut them in half, remove the seeds and slice. Sprinkle parsley on the tomatoes. Add to each plate some black olives, slices of yellow pepper, fried onion rings and a heap of carrots. To each plate add some toasted bread cubes. Sprinkle with a little olive oil and mix well.

Submitted in 1991 by the Sisters of the Italian Province
English translation: Frances Ruggeri Stephens from St. Louis, MO

School Sisters of Notre Dame
Celebrating **175** *years*

Orange-Almond Salad

Serves 6

6 cups leaf lettuce, torn
3 oranges, peeled, sliced crosswise and halved
1 cup celery, diced
1 small onion, chopped
⅓ cup almonds, toasted, slivered

Combine all ingredients in a large bowl.

Dressing:
¼ cup salad oil
2 tablespoons sugar
2 tablespoons cider vinegar
¼ teaspoon salt
⅛ teaspoon almond extract

57

Shake dressing ingredients well in a jar until sugar dissolves. Pour over salad just before serving.

Submitted in 1992 by Joan Bartosh, SSND from Rochester, MN

Upon being criticized for enjoying her food too much,

Teresa of Avila **exclaimed,**
when I pray, I pray!
when I partridge, I partridge!

School Sisters of Notre Dame
Celebrating **175** *years*

Orange-Chicken Salad

Serves 4

4 boneless, skinless chicken breasts, halved
2 cups chicken broth
1 garlic clove, smashed
1 pound green beans, trimmed, left whole

⅓ cup sour cream
2 teaspoons maple syrup
1 teaspoon lemon juice
¼ teaspoon salt
⅛ teaspoon pepper
Juice drained from can of mandarin oranges (optional)

58

1 (15-ounce) can mandarin oranges, drained
½ cup dried cranberries
1 head lettuce (or mixture of greens)
½ cup walnuts, chopped

Place chicken, broth and garlic in a large saucepan. Bring to a boil over medium-high heat; reduce to simmer. Cook until chicken is done, about 10 minutes, adding beans the last 5 minutes of cooking. Remove chicken to cutting board. Cool. Cut into strips.

To make the dressing stir together the sour cream, maple syrup, lemon juice, salt, pepper, and some of the reserved juice if desired. Combine chicken, beans, oranges, and dried cranberries. Gently toss with dressing. Line four plates with lettuce. Place a scoop of salad on top of lettuce, scatter chopped walnuts on top and serve.

Submitted by Janice Munier, SSND from St. Louis, MO

School Sisters of Notre Dame
Celebrating **175** *years*

Parmesan Vinaigrette Salad Dressing

Makes 2 cups

1 cup virgin olive oil
½ cup white balsamic vinegar
2 cloves garlic, crushed
2 tablespoons Parmesan cheese, grated
1 teaspoon Dijon mustard
¾ teaspoon salt
¾ teaspoon pepper
¼ teaspoon sugar
Dried thyme or dill or herbs of choice (optional)

Combine all ingredients in a jar with a tight-fitting lid. Shake well. **59**
Keeps for a couple of weeks in refrigerator.

Submitted by Maxine Pohlman, SSND from St. Louis, MO

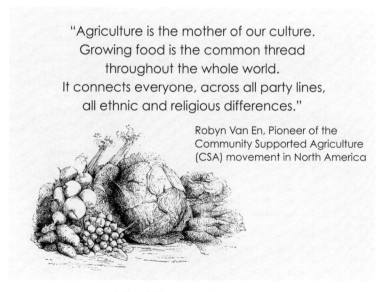

"Agriculture is the mother of our culture.
Growing food is the common thread
throughout the whole world.
It connects everyone, across all party lines,
all ethnic and religious differences."

Robyn Van En, Pioneer of the
Community Supported Agriculture
(CSA) movement in North America

School Sisters of Notre Dame
Celebrating **175** *years*

Refrigerator Dill Pickles

Makes 5 pint jars

4 to 6 heads dill, in small bunches
4 to 6 cloves garlic, cut into quarters
6 cups water
1 medium onion, cut into eighths
1 teaspoon dry mustard
2 cups white vinegar
½ cup salt
Cucumbers, enough to fill 5 pint jars, sliced or cut into spears

60

In an ice cream bucket or large bowl, mix all ingredients except the cucumbers. Let stand on the counter for three days uncovered. Then put cucumbers in jars and add mixture. Refrigerate.

Submitted by Adaire Lassonde, SSND from St. Paul, MN

Rich and Charlie's Salad

Serves 15-20

This recipe is from my niece, Michelle Jacquin.

1 head romaine lettuce
1 head iceberg lettuce
1 can artichoke hearts, drained
1 can hearts of palm, drained
1 jar pimentos, drained
1 large red onion, sliced

Dressing:
½ **cup Parmesan cheese**
½ **cup oil**
⅓ **cup vinegar**
Salt and pepper

61

Mix Parmesan cheese, oil and vinegar. Add salt and pepper to taste. Chill dressing. Tear lettuce into bowl and add chopped artichokes, hearts of palm, pimentos and sliced onion. Toss with dressing and serve.

Submitted by Odile Poliquin, SSND from St. Louis, MO

Rose's Italian Potato Salad

Serves 4

My mom, Rose Merlotti-Cassani, made a most delicious potato salad and created two variations that I am happy to share. All three potato salads are served best warm or at room temperature as are many Italian recipes.

8 small to medium potatoes
2 tablespoons fresh Italian parsley, snipped
1-2 cloves of garlic, crushed
Oil, canola or olive
Vinegar
Salt and pepper

62

Boil and peel the potatoes and chop them into small chunks. Add the parsley and the garlic. Drizzle oil over the potatoes and add several splashes of vinegar. Salt and pepper to taste.

Toss together and add more oil and vinegar if dry. To allow time for the flavors to mix before serving is a good thing.

Variation with beets:
To potatoes, garlic, oil and vinegar (omit parsley) add **3-4 fresh beets** cooked, peeled and chopped into chunks.

Variation with green beans:
To potatoes, garlic, oil and vinegar (parsley optional) add handfuls of **green beans** steamed and cut into small pieces.

Submitted by Gen Cassani, SSND from St. Louis, MO

School Sisters of Notre Dame
Celebrating **175** *years*

Kenya

Saladi (East African Salad Relish)

Serves 6

This salad relish is added to and mixed with hot spicy food by a guest, a little at a time to cool the spiciness of the dish and change its texture. If the hostess feels her dinner is not hot enough, a small hot chili pepper is added to the relish. She may also serve it individually or in a bowl with an additional piii-piii or hot pepper dissolved in lemon or tomato sauce.

2 cups cabbage, finely shredded
½ cup carrots, in very, very thin slices
½ cup sweet onions, cut fine
¼ cup green pepper, in fine strips

Combine in a 1-quart bowl. Fluff the mixture.
That's it. There is no dressing or seasoning.

Submitted by Janet Crane, SSND from Nairobi, Kenya

63

Each AMERICAN uses
153 GALLONS of WATER a day,
each BRITON uses
88 GALLONS of WATER a day,
each ASIAN uses **23 GALLONS,**
and *each AFRICAN uses* **12 GALLONS.**

Chile Peppers

Researchers estimate that **13 gallons per day**
is *the minimum needed* to sustain a human life.

Yes! Magazine, Winter 2004

School Sisters of Notre Dame
Celebrating **175** *years*

Spiced Tofu Salad with Apricot and Avocado

Serves 4

3 cups tofu, cubed, fried and salted
½ cup celery, thinly sliced
¼ cup green onions, thinly sliced
5 or 6 ripe apricots, sliced

3 tablespoons mayonnaise
3 tablespoons plain yogurt
1 tablespoon lemon juice
½ teaspoon lemon zest
½ teaspoon ground nutmeg

1 avocado, firm, ripe, peeled and seeded
2 tablespoons lime juice
¼ cup almonds, toasted, sliced
Lettuce leaves

In large bowl, lightly mix tofu, celery, onion and apricots. In small bowl, thoroughly mix mayonnaise, yogurt, lemon juice, zest and nutmeg. Combine with tofu mixture.

Slice avocado into small bowl; sprinkle with lime juice. Serve salad on lettuce leaves with almonds sprinkled on top and the avocado on the side.

NOTE: Chicken breast may be substituted for tofu.

Submitted by Suzanne Moynihan, SSND from Mount Calvary, WI

64

School Sisters of Notre Dame
Celebrating **175** *years*

Sunomono (Japanese Salad)

Sunomono with Cuttlefish and Cucumbers

Su means vinegar and Sunomono is a kind of AEMONO which is equivalent to a salad. Sunomono is also a very healthy food, always served cold and usually in small portions. Dressings contain such ingredients as vinegar, sugar, soy sauce, mirin (sweet sake), and sometimes sesame seeds and miso (soybean paste). The following is a true, typical sunomono which is often served at Japanese homes.

Serves 4

Cuttlefish or squid, fresh, skinned, **or any kind of white fish meat**

2-3 cucumbers

65

Cut the skinned cuttlefish into ¾ inch by 2 inch pieces. Boil in 2 cups water with a pinch of salt for about 20 seconds or until color partially changes. Drain well and cool. Peel cucumbers partially, put a little salt around them and roll them on a cutting board pushing them down. Slice into ¾ inch by 2 inch pieces, rinse salt off and drain well.

Dressing:
4 tablespoons vinegar
1 teaspoon ginger, fresh, grated
2 tablespoons soy sauce
1 tablespoon mirin (sweet sake)

Mix the ingredients for the dressing together.
Add the dressing to the cuttlefish and cucumbers just before serving.

Submitted by Janet Tanaka, SSND from Kyoto, Japan

Tessie's Cranberry Salad

Serves 16

3 (3-ounce) packages raspberry jello
3 cups boiling water
1 cup cold water
¾ cup port wine
1 cup cranberry sauce, whole berries
½ cup apples, chopped
½ cup pecans, chopped
1 (3-ounce) lemon jello
1 cup boiling water
½ cup mayonnaise
1 (4-ounce) container whipped topping

66

Dissolve raspberry jello in 3 cups boiling water. Add the cold water and wine. Chill until slightly thickened. Fold in cranberry sauce, apple and pecans. Pour into mold. Dissolve lemon jello in 1 cup boiling water. Chill until slightly thickened. Blend in mayonnaise and whipped topping. Pour over slightly thickened red jello.

Note: *To hasten thickening of raspberry jello, use 1 to 2 cups of ice in place of the one cup cold water. As it thickens, remove ice before it all melts. Speed up the thickening of the lemon jello by using ½ cup of ice and removing before completely melted.*

Submitted by Tessie Markus, SSND from Belleville, IL

Vegetable Salad

Serves 6-8

½ **head broccoli**
½ **head cauliflower**
¼ **cup black olives**, sliced
¼ **cup green olives**, sliced
1 **medium onion**, chopped
1 **green pepper**, diced
½ **cup oil**
3 **tablespoons lemon juice**
3 **teaspoons tarragon vinegar**
½ **teaspoon sugar**
¼ **teaspoon black pepper**
¾ **teaspoon salt**

67

Cut broccoli and cauliflower into bite-sized pieces and combine. Add black olives, green olives, onion and green pepper. Put the oil, lemon juice, tarragon vinegar, sugar, black pepper and salt into a covered bottle. Shake vigorously to dissolve sugar and blend. Pour over vegetables. Marinate at least 8 hours, stirring several times.

Other vegetables, such as radishes, tomatoes and zucchini, can be added or substituted.

Submitted in 1992 by Joan Bartosh, SSND from Rochester, MN

Water Lily Salad

This recipe appeared in a cookbook put together by the 1901 class of the Academy of Our Lady (A.O.L.) in 1925 to raise money for the chapel.

Remove shells from **hard-cooked eggs**. Cut eggs in halves either crosswise or lengthwise, cutting in such a way that the edges will be cut into sharp points. Remove yolk, mash and season with **salt, pepper** and **melted butter**, or moisten with **salad dressing**. Refill whites with yolks mixture and arrange halves on lettuce leaves. Serve with cooked salad dressing.

Submitted by Mary Charissia Powers, SSND (deceased)

68

Watergate Salad

Serves 10-15

1 (5-ounce) package pistachio instant pudding mix
1 (8-ounce) carton whipped topping
1 (20-ounce) can crushed pineapple
1 cup miniature marshmallows
1 cup nuts, chopped

Combine pudding mix and whipped topping. Add pineapple, marshmallows and nuts. Stir well. Pour into 9x13 inch casserole. Serve.

Submitted in 1993 by Marie Torno, SSND from Chatawa, MS

69

Why Buy Local Fruits and Vegetables?

Freshness: they are often harvested within 24 hours before purchase.

Taste: produce picked before it ripens so it can be shipped a great distance will not develop the sugars, acids, and volatiles that enhance flavor.

Nutrition: nutritional value declines as time passes.

Regional economic health: keeping money within the community contributes to the health and sustainability of the local economy.

Energy conservation: less fuel is used for long-distance distribution.

Farmland preservation: farmers need to be economically viable to preserve the unique culture and beautiful scenery of farming communities.

School Sisters of Notre Dame
Celebrating **175** *years*

Strawberry Patch

by Maura Eichner, SSND

These days are circumscribed with sun—
now cool, damp May is over,
and the fields are rich, sweet purple,
grown hand-high in hills of clover.
Here on the sandy sloping fields
sprawl rows and rows of berries
flushed to the same deep purple-red
of the orchard's ripened cherries.
Light and harmonious hums explore
the thick, low shrubs, and tiny things
dart out in small ecstatic leaps
on delicate translucent wings.

Then take the weary heart in Spring
to young farm hills of Thabor
and kneeling see God manifest,
and learn the dignity of labor.

SIDE DISHES

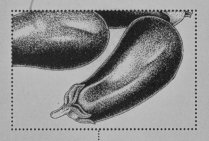

Blessed Theresa writes:

To Reverend D. Andrew Paulatig
of Gorizia, Italy

We heartily thank you, reverend Director, for
your kind offer concerning the sending of honey.
I was most pleasantly surprised on my return
from a recent journey to find the beautiful
peaches, pomegranates, and excellent lemons
which your love sent us. We can really give
nothing in return but a hearty "May God reward
you." Munich, October 19, 1875 (#3955)

Brussels Sprouts and Sweet Potatoes

Serves 4

2 tablespoons pecan pieces
1½ **cups sweet potatoes,** peeled, cubed
¾ **pound brussels sprouts,** halved
1 **tablespoon butter or margarine**
½ **cup onion,** chopped
1 **teaspoon fresh garlic,** crushed
¼ **cup chicken stock**
4 **teaspoons brown sugar or honey**
¼ **teaspoon cinnamon**

74

Toast pecans. To toast pecans stir in a dry skillet over medium heat for 2 minutes until brown. Set aside. Bring saucepan of water to a boil, add sweet potatoes and cook for 3-5 minutes or until tender. Remove with slotted spoon. Set aside. Return water to a boil, add brussels sprouts and cook until tender. Set aside. Melt margarine in skillet, sauté onions and garlic until tender. Add potatoes, sprouts, chicken stock, sugar, cinnamon and pecans. Cook 3 minutes.

Submitted by Gen Cassani, SSND from St. Louis, MO

Corn Pudding

Serves 8

¼ **cup margarine**
½ **cup sugar**
4 eggs, slightly beaten
2 (16-ounce) cans cream-style corn
½ **cup flour**
1 teaspoon baking powder

Cream the margarine and sugar. Mix in eggs. Stir in corn, then the flour, and finally the baking powder. Pour into a 2-quart oven-proof bowl. Bake in 350 degree oven for one hour or until brown and solidified in the middle.

75

Submitted by John Vianney Zullo, SSND from Bridgeport, CT

Corn Souffle

Serves 8-10

½ **cup butter or margarine,** melted in a casserole dish
2 eggs
4 tablespoons sugar
3 tablespoons flour
1 (16-ounce) can whole corn, drained
1 (16-ounce) can creamed corn

In a casserole dish, whip together margarine, eggs, sugar and flour. Then mix in corn. Bake at 350 degrees for 45 minutes (uncovered).

76

Submitted by Rita Marie Schneider, SSND from Mankato, MN

*How we eat determines
to a considerable extent
how the world is used.*

Wendell Berry

Crunchy Potato Casserole

Serves 8-10

6-8 potatoes, cleaned and quartered
½ cup sour cream
3 tablespoons butter or margarine
1 egg
1 tablespoon onion, chopped
Salt and pepper, to taste
Milk, as needed

Cook potatoes until tender. Add the sour cream, butter and egg.
Beat until fluffy. Add onions, salt, pepper and, if necessary, milk.
Put into a greased casserole dish.

77

Topping:
¼ cup cornflakes or Rice Krispies
¼ cup cheese, grated
1½ tablespoons butter or margarine

Mix together cereal, cheese and butter. Sprinkle on top of
casserole. Bake for 30 minutes at 350 degrees.

Submitted in 1993 by Mary Eric Militzer, SSND from Milwaukee, WI

Drinking Bread (Nanburu)

Serves 20

A favorite dish for Good Friday.

5 cups uncooked rice, pounded into a powder
¼ bowl baobab fruit
Sugar, to taste
3 bananas, sliced
Flavoring essence (your choice)
½ cup coconut
1 small can milk (optional)

78 Make the rice powder into small balls using a little hot water to make it stick together. Steam the rice powder balls. Soak ¼ bowl of baobab fruit in water for 1 hour. Sieve the baobab. Add sugar and essence to taste. Mix the already steamed rice with the baobab until it is well mixed. Add the sliced bananas, coconut or milk as you like.

Submitted by the Sisters of The Gambia

The Gambia **is a sliver in the side of West Africa and one of its tiniest countries.**

If you travel in the remote deserts of Australia, Africa or Madagascar, you may from time to time spot a solitary tree that looks as if it is growing upside-down, with gnarled roots sitting atop a huge, smooth, trunk. This is the Baobab Tree.

The baobab fruit has a furry coating around a tough, gourd-like shell that shields a soft pulp inside called 'monkey bread' and seeds that are rich in citric acid and oil.

School Sisters of Notre Dame
Celebrating **175** *years*

Easy Corn Casserole

Serves 8-10

A tradition in our family at Thanksgiving and Christmas.

1 package corn muffin mix
1 (16-ounce) can whole or creamed corn
½ (16-ounce) package corn, frozen
4 ounces sour cream
½ teaspoon Mrs. Dash seasoning
1 tablespoon margarine, melted
1 cup mozzarella cheese, shredded

Mix all ingredients together and bake covered at 350 degrees for **79** one hour.

Submitted by Marilyn Wussler, SSND from St Louis, MO.

Eggplant Parmesan

Revised and Nutritious

Serves 4

1 medium to large eggplant, peeled and sliced in ⅜ inch slices
Milk, enough to cover eggplant
4 tablespoons sesame seeds, toasted
1-2 carrots, grated
½ cup Parmesan cheese
2 cups spaghetti sauce
1 cup mozzarella cheese, shredded

80

Soak the eggplant slices in milk to rid them of bitterness. While they are soaking, prepare a 6X9 inch baking dish with cooking spray. Toast sesame seeds in small frying pan over medium heat until fragrant and turning color.

Mix together grated carrots, Parmesan cheese and sauce. Heat through. Add seeds just before layering in the baking dish.

Take eggplant out of the milk and drip-dry on a paper towel. Put a single layer of eggplant in the baking dish. Spread half the sauce mixture on it and sprinkle some mozzarella cheese on top of this layer. Repeat with remaining eggplant, sauce and cheese. Bake at 350 degrees, about 20 minutes, until eggplant is tender when stuck with a fork.

Submitted by Carol Marie Hemish, SSND from Buffalo, MN

Farina Dumplings

Serves 4

This recipe appeared in a cookbook put together by the 1901 class of the Academy of Our Lady (A.O.L.) in 1925 to raise money for the chapel.

1 cup water
1 cup milk

When boiling stir in
½ cup farina

Cook until thick. Add
Piece of butter the size of a walnut
Salt
Pepper
Ginger

81

When cold add the yolks of **4 eggs**

Submitted by Sister Mary Castula, SSND from Milwaukee, WI (deceased)

Fried Potatoes

Serves 2-3

1 pound potatoes
8 ounces oil

Wash the potatoes. After peeling the potatoes, cut them like matchsticks. Dry them on paper towels. Heat the oil in a deep skillet or pot. Drop the cut-up potatoes into boiling oil a few at a time. After they have browned, lift them out with a strainer. Drain them on paper towels and arrange them on a plate covered with a napkin. Serve the potatoes warm. They can be salted at the table.

Note: *Never leave boiling oil unattended.*

Submitted in 1991 by the Sisters of the Italian Province
English translation: Frances Ruggeri Stephens from St. Louis, MO

82

Time

Eating locally means eating with the rhythm of the seasons.

"Slow food" helps us savor God's gifts of nourishment. And it just tastes good!

Finding creative ways to eat together and share food strengthens community bonds and adds joy to our lives.

Simply in Season Study Guide
www.worldcommunitycookbook.org/season/studyguide.html

School Sisters *of* Notre Dame
Celebrating **175** *years*

Glazed Carrots

Serves 6

10 to 12 medium or small carrots, washed and peeled
Salt
2 tablespoons butter or margarine
¾ cups sugar
1 small bottle or can of 7-up

Cook the carrots in water with a little salt. Take out before
completely tender. Mix together in a skillet butter, sugar and 7-up.
Cook over medium heat, stirring until sugar is dissolved and butter
melted. Place carrots in skillet; cover and let simmer until carrots
are done and glazed. Do not overcook.

83

Submitted in 1993 by Leocadia Meyer, SSND from St. Louis, MO (deceased)

The principles of **Slow Food** are:

- choosing locally grown and produced items,
- preparing them in traditinal ways, and
- eating with friends and family.

To learn more about Slow Food, visit www.slowfoodusa.org

School Sisters of Notre Dame
Celebrating **175** *years*

Homemade Noodles

Mother would have the kitchen table all spread out with her homemade noodles, for drying. They dried all day long. Then, she would seal them in gallon glass containers for future use. I can still see her happy smile when we were so excited to see them all over the table.

3 egg yolks and 1 whole egg
3 tablespoons cold water
1 teaspoon salt
2 cups flour, sifted

Beat yolks and whole egg until very light. Beat in the cold water and salt. Stir flour into mixture and work with hands until blended. Divide dough into two parts. On lightly floured board, roll out each piece as thin as possible. Let lay until dough is partially dry. Roll up as for jelly roll. With a thin sharp knife, cut into strips of desired width (⅛ inch for fine, ½ inch for broad). Shake out the strips and allow to dry before using or storing.

Submitted by Bernelle Taube, SSND from Northfield, MN

84

In this food, I see clearly the presence of the entire universe supporting my existence.
Thich Nhat Hanh

Indian Fried Eggplant

Serves 3-4

1 medium eggplant
½ **cup flour**
1 egg
½ **cup milk**
1 teaspoon curry powder
½ **teaspoon baking powder**
½ **teaspoon turmeric** (optional)
1 teaspoon oil
Oil for deep frying

Wash eggplant. Cut into ½ inch slices. Set aside. To make the batter, place remaining ingredients in a bowl and beat with rotary beater until smooth. Heat one inch deep oil to 375 degrees in large skillet. Dip slices into batter, letting excess drip into bowl. Fry slices in hot oil until golden brown, turning once. Drain. Salt and pepper to taste.

85

Submitted by Mary Beck, SSND from Mount Calvary, WI

School Sisters of Notre Dame
Celebrating **175** *years*

Lima Bean Casserole

Serves 4

2 cups dried lima beans
2 cups onions, chopped
1 tablespoon oil
¼ pound cheese, grated
½ teaspoon salt
1 cup nuts, chopped

Soak beans in water overnight, then drain, and cook in fresh water until tender. In another pot, sauté onions in oil. Add beans, cheese and salt, stir together. Bake for an hour in warm oven. If desired add more oil and stir. Sprinkle top with nuts.

Submitted by Suzanne Moynihan, SSND from Mount Calvary, WI

86

GET TO KNOW A FARMER.
VISIT A FARM.

Support a farming family by shopping at a Farmers' Market.

Be sure to ask sellers where their produce
is grown because not all farmers' markets sell local food.

School Sisters of Notre Dame
Celebrating **175** *years*

Mama Mercurio's Green Beans and Potato Salad

Serves 4-6

This is a wonderful summer meal. Tuna or crab meat may be added or even fresh home-grown tomatoes. And so healthy . . .

1 pound fresh green beans
12 small red potatoes
Olive oil
Vinegar
Salt and pepper, to taste
Minced garlic, to taste

Clean and cook the green beans. At the same time but in a separate pot, cook red potatoes. Cut potatoes in half. Cut beans in half or thirds. Place potatoes and beans in a bowl and splash with olive oil and vinegar. Salt and pepper to taste. Stir in garlic. Substitute Italian Dressing for olive oil and vinegar if desired.

Submitted by Rose Mercurio, SSND from St. Louis, MO

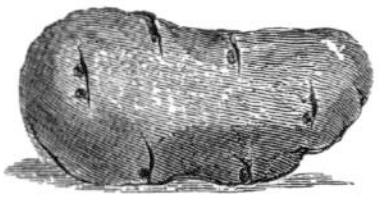

See what is
IN SEASON
where you live.

Visit a farmers' market near you. If you live in the USA, you can find a farmer's market by going to:
www.farmersmarketsusa.org/

Melanzane Alla Parmigiana (Eggplant Parmesan)

Serves 5-6

From Sister Kenneth Marie Kozal's collection of Italian recipes.

Note: *Prepare eggplant and sauce 1 to 8 hours ahead.*

2 pounds eggplant
Olive oil
1 cup Parmesan cheese, grated
1 pound mozzarella, shredded
2 cups freshly made tomato sauce (use Roma tomatoes)
Flour
2-4 tablespoons fresh basil, chopped
Salt and pepper, to taste

88

Peel the eggplant and cut into ¼ inch slices. Salt them and put them in a colander to drain for an hour or more. This takes the bitterness away from the eggplant. Dip the slices in flour and either fry them lightly in a little olive oil or bake them in a dish coated with a little olive oil at 350 degrees for about 10 minutes each side or until soft.

To make the tomato sauce, take Roma tomatoes, peel and cube. Simmer with basil until tender. In an oven dish, layer tomato sauce, eggplant slices, mozzarella and Parmesan cheese until all ingredients are used. Finish with a little Parmesan. Put it in the oven at 400 degrees for 20-30 minutes until a golden crust forms.

Submitted by Mary Beck, SSND from Mount Calvary, WI

Mexican Corn

Serves 6-8

8 ounces cream cheese
2 tablespoons butter or margarine
¼ cup milk
¼ teaspoon garlic salt
2 cans whole kernel corn, drained
2 small cans green chilies, chopped

Melt cream cheese and butter in milk and garlic salt over low heat. Add corn and chilies. Put in casserole and bake uncovered at 350 degrees for 20-25 minutes.

Submitted in 1993 by Marie Torno, SSND from Chatawa, MS

89

In Iowa, the nation's leading corn producer, corn has traveled an average of 1,426 miles to the grocery-store shelves,

compared with 20 miles for locally grown corn.

THE RESULT? As much as 17 times more fossil fuel used and carbon dioxide emitted.

Leopold Center for Sustainable Agriculture
www.leopold.iastate.edu

School Sisters of Notre Dame
Celebrating **175** *years*

Mexican Rice

Serves 6-8

2 cups rice, uncooked
½ cup oil
2 green onions with tops, chopped
½ green pepper, chopped
1 tomato, thinly sliced
½ cup tomato sauce
½ teaspoon pepper
½ teaspoon garlic powder
Salt, to taste
¼ teaspoon cumin
3½ cups chicken broth
1 (10 ounce) package peas, frozen

90

Heat rice in oil until golden. Add remaining ingredients and stir. Cover and cook over low heat about 20 minutes or until rice is tender and most of the liquid is absorbed.

Submitted in 1993 by Marie Torno, SSND from Chatawa, MS

Millionaire's Spinach

Serves 4

1 pound bag fresh spinach
½ **onion**, chopped
2 tablespoons butter or margarine
1 cup cold milk
¼ teaspoon salt
½ teaspoon pepper
2 tablespoons cornstarch

Cut up spinach, cook, drain very well. Set aside. Sauté onion in
the butter until done (translucent). Add salt and pepper. Mix milk
and cornstarch. Add to onion mixture. Bring to a boil. Stirring
constantly, boil one minute. Mix with the well-drained spinach.
Serve hot.

91

Submitted in 1993 by Marie Torno, SSND from Chatawa, MS

**Studies show that food loses nutritional value
as time passes, so a head of spinach
that was picked the day before
purchase is actually more
nutritious than the one
that has spent two weeks
in trucks and warehouses.**

Audubon Magazine 3 - 2006

School Sisters of Notre Dame
Celebrating **175** *years*

Mom Scheurer's Potato Salad

Serves 25

Almost every Sunday during the summer, our family made this recipe
to take to the lake for supper. There were nine of us plus Mom, Dad,
Grandma and almost always friends and neighbors. My Dad would also
buy 10 pounds of home-made hot dogs, and grill them on a flat grill . . . in
butter . . . Mmmm, Good!

10 pounds cooked potatoes, thinly sliced
1 dozen eggs, hard-cooked, thinly sliced
1 stalk celery, sliced
1 medium onion, sliced
1 jar mayonnaise, to your taste
1 cup yellow prepared mustard, to your taste
1 cup cream or milk, to your taste
1 tablespoon sugar, to your taste
Salt and pepper, to your taste

Mix all of this together and be sure that it is very moist. If you need
to add more mayonnaise or cream, do so.

Submitted by Katherine Scheurer, SSND from Mankato, MN

92

Mother's Baked Beans

Serves 10

My mother's recipe that I love to make.

2 cups navy beans
½ teaspoon baking soda
1 tablespoon molasses
¼ cup brown sugar
1 to 2 teaspoons salt
½ teaspoon dry mustard
½ teaspoon pepper
¼ pound salt pork
1 onion, minced

93

In a pot, soak navy beans in water overnight. In the morning let them come to a boil then add baking soda and boil 15 minutes. Drain. Add fresh water to cover beans. Mix in the rest of ingredients. Put into casserole and bake at 350 degrees about 4 hours until it boils, then at 250 degrees until it is done, about 2 hours longer.

Submitted by Bernelle Taube, SSND from Northfield, MN

Mushrooms with Parsley and Garlic

Serves 6

1½ **pounds small white mushrooms**
2 **tablespoons butter or margarine**
2 **tablespoons olive oil**
¼ **cup parsley**, chopped
3 **garlic cloves**, chopped
Salt and pepper, to taste

Wipe mushrooms with a damp cloth. Cut into slices. Melt butter with oil in a large skillet. When butter foams, add mushrooms. Sauté over high heat until golden. Add parsley, garlic, salt and pepper, and cook one minute longer. Taste and adjust for seasoning. Serve hot or at room temperature.

Submitted in 1993 by Marie Torno, SSND from Chatawa, MS

94

Peacock Vegetables

Serves 6

2 red onions, cut into eighths
2 small yellow squash, cut into ½ inch strips
2 small zucchini, cut into ½ inch strips
1 red bell pepper, cut into ½ inch strips
1 green bell pepper, cut into ½ inch strips
1 yellow bell pepper, cut into ½ inch strips
4 cloves garlic, sliced thin
2 tablespoons fresh parsley, minced
1 tablespoon balsamic vinegar
1 tablespoon olive oil
½ teaspoon dried oregano
¼ teaspoon salt
¼ teaspoon ground black pepper

95

Preheat oven to 425 degrees. Place onions, yellow squash,
zucchini, bell peppers and garlic in a bowl and toss well.
Combine parsley, vinegar, oil, oregano, salt and black pepper
in a lidded jar; shake well. Pour over vegetables; toss to coat.
Spoon into a greased 9x13 inch baking pan. Bake 20 minutes,
stirring every 5 minutes. Serve warm or at room temperature.

Submitted by Shelley Hogan, SSND from St. Louis, MO

Peggy's Delicious Rice

Serves 6

1 onion, chopped
½ cup butter or margarine
1 cup rice, uncooked
2 (10½-ounce) cans beef broth

Sauté onion in butter or margarine. Place uncooked rice in oven-proof casserole. Add the onion. Cover with beef broth. Stir well. Bake uncovered for one hour at 375 degrees.

Submitted by Betty Sweeney, SSND Associate from Baltimore, MD

96

Phyllis's Pasta Con Broccoli

Serves 4-6

This was a favorite Friday meal at our home. Sometimes, Mom would take the larger pieces of broccoli out and scramble them with eggs and make a "pie."

1 onion, chopped
2 cloves of garlic, minced
4 tablespoons olive oil
2 quarts water
1 bunch fresh broccoli (frozen may be substituted)
½ pound angel hair pasta

97

In a pot, brown onion and garlic in olive oil until onion is translucent. Pour in water and bring to a boil. Break broccoli into small pieces and cook until tender (*al dente*, not mushy). Break pasta in half and cook in boiling broccoli and water until done. Salt and pepper to taste. Serve in soup size bowl. May be topped with grated Parmesan cheese. Mmmm, now that's Italian!

Variations:
You may substitute cauliflower or asparagus for broccoli.

Submitted by Rose Mercurio, SSND from St. Louis, MO

School Sisters of Notre Dame
Celebrating **175** *years*

Posole

Serves 20

In the South Southwest, at Christmas time or when one is hosting a celebration, posole is served. This is a sign of hospitality. It is influenced by the Pueblo and Spanish cultures. Posole is the Spanish word for hominy.

Posole can be made without meat. Some prefer using trimmed pork steaks. The Posole can be found in cans. The people in New Mexico prefer to get the whole hominy.

2 or 3 lean pork steaks (optional)
2 pints canned posole/hominy or 1 bag whole hominy, soaked in water overnight
1 cup mild red chili
5-6 garlic cloves, chopped or pressed
1 tablespoon oregano, whole
1 or 2 lemons or limes
1 onion, chopped (optional)

98

If using meat, cut into pieces and cook in water at medium heat until done. Keep broth. In a large pan of water, put crushed garlic and posole. Bring to boil, then lower heat. Add water if necessary since some posole tends to absorb the water. When posole is tender, add cooked meat, the broth and oregano. Add mild red chili as desired. Just before serving, squeeze juice from the limes or lemons into the posole. Chopped raw onion can also be added on top.

Submitted by Dolorette Farias, SSND from Houston, TX

Potato Salad

Serves 5-8

1¼ cups Italian dressing or vinaigrette
5-8 large potatoes, cubed, cooked, salted
1 cup celery, chopped
¼ cup onion, shredded
4-6 eggs, hard cooked, peeled and sliced
¼ cup carrots, shredded
¼ cup radishes, shredded
½ cup mayonnaise
¼ cup French Dijon mustard

99

Pour dressing over warm potatoes and chill for 1 to 2 hours.
Add celery, onion, eggs, carrots and radishes to the potatoes.
Mix the mayonnaise and mustard. Add to the potato mixture.
Chill for 2-4 hours. Serve.

Submitted by Margaret Karas, SSND from Greenfield, WI

**Every blade of grass, *(every fruit and vegetable)* has an
angel leaning over it, whispering,**

"Grow! Grow!"
The Talmud

Radishes

School Sisters of Notre Dame
Celebrating **175** *years*

Potatoes Supreme

Serves 8-10

Note: Dish may be frozen and baked at a later date.

1 (2-pound) package frozen hash browns
1 (10-ounce) can cream of chicken soup
1 (8-ounce) stick sharp cheddar cheese, shredded
1 (16-ounce) container sour cream
1 cup onions, diced
½ cup margarine, melted
Salt and pepper, to taste
1 cup potato chips or corn flakes, crushed

100

Let hash browns thaw for 30 minutes. Combine first seven ingredients. Mix well. Put in 9x13 inch casserole pan. Top with crushed chips or corn flakes. Bake uncovered at 350 degrees for 35 to 45 minutes.

Submitted by Margaret Karas, SSND from Greenfield, WI

Pumpkin Risotto

Serves 6-8

Note: Butternut squash may be substituted for pumpkin.

6 cups vegetable stock
2 cups pumpkin puree
2 tablespoons extra virgin olive oil
⅔ cup onions, caramelized
2 cups Arborio rice (sweet brown rice also works)
1 teaspoon fresh rosemary, minced
2 tablespoons fresh sage, minced
½ cup white wine
2 tablespoons butter
½ cup Parmesan cheese, grated
Salt and pepper, to taste

101

In a large saucepan over medium heat, whisk together the stock and pumpkin puree. Bring just to a simmer for 10 minutes, maintain over low heat. In a large saucepan over medium heat, warm the olive oil. Add the caramelized onions and rice and stir until the grains are well coated with the oil and are nearly translucent, about 3 minutes. Stir in the rosemary and sage. Add the wine and stir until it is absorbed. Add the simmering stock mixture to the rice mixture one ladleful at a time. Stir frequently after each addition. Wait until the stock is almost completely absorbed before adding more.

When rice is tender to the bite and looks creamy *(after about 30 minutes)* stir in the butter, cheese, salt and pepper. Serve immediately.

(continued on next page)

School Sisters of Notre Dame
Celebrating **175** *years*

Note: To caramelize onions, sauté the onions in oil over medium-high heat until tender (about 3 minutes). Add about a teaspoon brown sugar for each onion used and mix well. Continue cooking, stirring occasionally, for 7-10 minutes, or until the onions are a light caramel color.

Submitted by Maxine Pohlman, SSND from St. Louis, MO

All food has a story

All food has a story.
It comes to us through
a "food (production) chain"
of people and places—
a chain that is growing
increasingly long.

> Eating is a spiritual act,
> because our food choices
> affect everyone in this chain:
> God's children and God's
> creation.

Shortening our chain—by choosing local,
seasonal food—
introduces joyful rhythms into our everyday
lives, and is a way to address world problems
that seem overwhelming.

Simply in Season Study Guide
www.worldcommunitycookbook.org/season/studyguide.html

School Sisters *of* Notre Dame
Celebrating **175** *years*

Ravioli with Tomatoes, White Beans, and Escarole

Serves 6-8

1 (9-ounce) package fresh four-cheese ravioli
1 (15-ounce) can great northern or navy beans, rinsed and drained
1 (14 –ounce) can diced tomatoes, undrained
½ teaspoon basil, dried
½ teaspoon oregano, dried
⅛ teaspoon red pepper, crushed
6 cups escarole or spinach, fresh, chopped
¼ cup water
¼ cup Asiago cheese, grated

103

Cook pasta according to package directions, omitting salt and fat. Combine beans, tomatoes, basil, oregano, and red pepper in a large saucepan. Bring to a boil; stir in escarole. Cover, reduce heat, and simmer 3 minutes or until escarole is wilted. Stir in pasta and water. Cook 1 minute or until thoroughly heated. Sprinkle with cheese and serve.

Submitted by Shelley Hogan, SSND from St. Louis, MO

Try eating **your colors** *every day.*
red • green • orange • yellow • white • purple

School Sisters of Notre Dame
Celebrating **175** *years*

Rice and Beans

Serves 6

This can also be a main dish.

½ **cup dry black beans**
1½ **cups brown rice,** uncooked
1 **tablespoon chili powder**
3 **cloves garlic,** minced
2 **cups onion,** chopped
1 **cup green pepper,** chopped
½ **cup ketchup**
3 **cups mozzarella cheese,** grated
104 1 **cup cottage cheese**
Cheddar cheese, grated

Cover beans in water and let soak overnight. Cook for 1½ hours. Drain and discard the water. Cook rice in 3 cups water in a covered saucepan for 40 minutes or until tender. Mix cooked beans and rice together with everything except cheeses. Mix the mozzarella and cottage cheese together. In a greased baking dish, layer bean and rice mixture with cheese mixture. Top layer should be bean and rice mixture. Bake 30 minutes at 350 degrees. Sprinkle with grated cheddar cheese before serving.

Submitted by Dorothy Olinger, SSND from St. Paul, MN

Risotto a la Milanese

Serves 4 – 6

Sunday's midday meal was often this creamy risotto. I learned to make risotto watching my mom and her sister, my aunt, at the stove. They helped me see how a sense of timing is important in creating this rather simple and ordinary Northern Italian dish, which now appears on the menus of many restaurants. The key to risotto is moderate boiling, constantly stirring, and adding the right amount of broth.

Porcini mushrooms (optional but adds a delicious flavor)
6 tablespoons butter
1 large onion, finely sliced and chopped
2 cups Arborio rice
½ cup white or red wine
8-10 cups chicken broth (you may not need all of it)
1-2 envelopes or capsules saffron
Parmesan or asiago cheese

105

Clean a handful of dried mushrooms by rinsing in water and then soak them in enough hot water to cover them. You can use other mushrooms but the flavor will be different.

In a heavy bottom saucepan or dutch oven, sauté the butter and onions until golden brown—not burnt but close. Add the rice stirring constantly until the rice is coated.

Add the wine and enough chicken broth to cover the rice by about one inch, while constantly stirring. Add more broth as needed, about ½ cup at a time, allowing each ½ cup to be absorbed before adding another, but leaving the rice always moist.

(continued on next page)

School Sisters of Notre Dame
Celebrating **175** *years*

After about 15 minutes of constantly stirring and adding broth, begin to test the rice. It should be *al dente*. Once the rice has absorbed enough broth that it looks thick and tastes *al dente (a little hard to the tooth)*, drain the porcini mushrooms and add to the risotto. Add another tablespoon or two of butter (optional).

If you are unable to find porcini, add chopped steamed asparagus or pieces of chicken or just savor risotto plain. Sprinkle with grated Parmesan or asiago cheese.

Buon appetito!

Submitted by Gen Cassani, SSND from St. Louis, MO

106

Skillet Zucchini

Serves 4-6

1 stalk celery, chopped
¼ cup onion, chopped
1 tablespoon canola oil

Place in frying pan and sauté about 5 minutes or until tender.
Then add:

3 medium zucchini, quartered lengthwise and then cut into
½ inch pieces
2 tomatoes, cut in eighths
2 tablespoons ketchup
Salt and pepper, to taste

107

Cook about 10 minutes, stirring occasionally, until zucchini is
tender.

Submitted by Joan Bartosh, SSND from Rochester, MN

Spinach Casserole

Serves 4

This recipe is from my sister, Odile Lampe.

2 cups cottage cheese (small curd)
3 eggs, beaten
¼ cup margarine, cut into small pieces
¼ teaspoon pepper
¼ pound longhorn cheese (mild cheddar or Colby), cut into pieces
2 packages frozen spinach, chopped, thawed and drained
3 heaping tablespoons flour

108

Mix all ingredients together. Put into a greased casserole dish and leave uncovered. Bake 350 degrees for 1 hour.

Submitted by Odile Poliquin, SSND from St. Louis, MO

Every convent
should have
a garden.
Mother Theresa Gerhardinger

School Sisters of Notre Dame
Celebrating **175** *years*

Stewed Peas

Serves 3-4

Butter
1 bunch parsley, chopped
1 can peas, drained
Salt and pepper

In a frying pan, brown the butter and parsley for a few minutes. Add the peas; then salt and pepper to taste. Let them simmer over a moderate flame until heated through.

Submitted in 1991 by the Sisters of the Italian Province
English Translation: Frances Ruggeri Stephens from St. Louis, MO

109

Stuffed Eggplant

Serves 8-10

4 eggplants
3 tablespoons olive oil
Pepperoncini, chopped
1 clove garlic, smashed
1 pound tomatoes, peeled, diced or chopped
3 peppers, cut finely
Basil
Salt
Oil

110

Cut the eggplants lengthwise, sprinkle the pulp with salt then let
them rest for at least an hour. Using a spoon, scoop out the inside
of the eggplants and put them in an oiled baking dish. Dice
the pulp that was extracted from the eggplants. Season with
3 tablespoons of olive oil, add the chopped pepperoncini let set
for 15 minutes. Mix in the garlic, tomatoes and peppers. Season
with basil and salt. Stuff the eggplants with the mixture. Sprinkle
with a little oil and bake at 350 degrees for about an hour.

Submitted in 1991 by the Sisters of the Italian Province
English Translation: Frances Ruggeri Stephens from St. Louis, MO

School Sisters of Notre Dame
Celebrating **175** *years*

Stuffed Potatoes

Serves 4-6

6 large, round potatoes
6 eggs
Cheese, grated
6 slices bread, crusts removed
Butter or margarine
Salt
Pepper

Bake the potatoes in a low (325 degrees) oven, until they can be easily pierced by a fork (about 1 hour). Remove the potatoes from the oven and cut off the tops. With a spoon, scoop out most of the pulp and put it in a bowl; season with salt and pepper, and mash. Stuff the hollowed potatoes with the mashed pulp leaving openings at the tops. Break the eggs into the potato openings, taking care not to break the yolk. Sprinkle with grated cheese, season with salt and pepper and cover with bread. Put the potatoes back into the oven. When the grated cheese browns, the potatoes are ready. Serve hot.

111

Submitted by Jovann Irrgang, SSND from Dallas, TX

Tangy Green Beans

Serves 7-9

1½ **pounds fresh green beans**, trimmed
⅓ **cup sweet red pepper**, diced
4½ **teaspoons olive oil**
4½ **teaspoons water**
1½ **teaspoons white wine vinegar or cider vinegar**
1½ **teaspoons spicy brown mustard**
¾ **teaspoon salt**
¼ **teaspoon pepper**
⅛ **teaspoon garlic powder**

112

In a saucepan, place beans and red pepper in a basket over
1 inch of boiling water. Cover and steam for 7-8 minutes or until
crisp-tender. Meanwhile, in a bowl, whisk together the remaining
ingredients. Transfer bean mixture to a serving bowl; add whisked
vinaigrette and stir to coat.

Submitted by Shelly Hogan, SSND from St. Louis, MO

Tomatoes Stuffed
with Egg and Peppers

This recipe appeared in a cookbook put together by the 1901 class of the Academy of Our Lady (A.O.L.) in 1925 to raise money for the chapel.

Cut the inside from large solid tomatoes and refill with a mixture of equal parts of:

Chopped **hard-boiled eggs**
Chopped **sweet green peppers**

Moisten well with melted **butter, onion juice** and season with **salt**.

Put in a baking dish, cover, and let bake for twenty minutes in a moderate oven. Tomatoes may be stuffed in a great variety of ways, using fillings of chopped onion, fried cucumber, spinach or bread dressing with sage, etc.

Submitted by M. Castula, SSND from Milwaukee, WI (deceased)

Twice-Baked Potatoes

Serves 4

2 potatoes
3 tablespoons skim milk
1 teaspoon Parmesan cheese
2 teaspoon onion, minced
2 tablespoons nonfat plain yogurt
Paprika

Bake potatoes at 375 degrees until done, about 1 hour. Then, scoop out the insides leaving a shell. Whip the potato pulp and add milk, Parmesan, onion and yogurt. Refill the potato shells and sprinkle paprika on top. Bake potatoes again till they are piping hot, about 30 minutes, in a 350 degree oven.

Submitted in 1993 by Mariel Kreuziger, SSND from Coolville, OH

114

Walla-Walla Treat

Serves 1-2

Large sweet onion
Butter or margarine
Granular chicken or beef bouillon

Slice the one onion like a pie but not all the way through so it
opens like a flower. Put a pat of margarine in the center with a
sprinkling of granular chicken or beef bouillon. Close up the onion
and wrap tightly with foil. Bake at 350 degrees for about an hour.

Yum, yum.

115

Submitted by Mary Beck, SSND from Mount Calvary, WI

Whipped Sweet Potatoes
in Orange Shells

1947
COOKBOOK

Serves 8

This recipe appeared in the Notre Dame centenary Cookbook put together by our wonderful "cook" sisters in 1947.

8 Sunkist oranges
4 cups boiled or baked sweet potatoes
2 teaspoons salt
2 tablespoons butter, melted
8 marshmallows

116

Cut of tops of oranges and remove pulp and juice with a sharp knife and spoon. Whip sweet potatoes with salt, butter and orange juice to moisten to desired consistency. Use juice secured in preparing shells. Fill orange shells and top each with a marshmallow. Brown in moderate oven until heated through.

Submitted by M. Dora, SSND from New England, ND

Winter Squash

Serves 4

1 winter squash (about 2 cups)
1 apple, sliced
½ cup raisins
½ cup orange juice
Marshmallows

Bake squash in a 350 degree oven until soft (about an hour) and scoop out pulp. In a casserole dish, mash the pulp and add the apple, raisins and orange juice. Top with marshmallows. Reheat until piping hot and apples have baked, about 30 minutes in a 350 degree oven.

117

Submitted in 1993 by Mariel Kreuziger, SSND from Coolville, OH

Yummy Summer Squash

Summer squash
Butter or margarine, melted
Parmesan cheese
Oregano
Parsley

Slice squash in half. Into a baking pan pour about ¼ inch hot water and place in it the squash, cut side down. Bake covered at 350 degrees for ½ hour. Drain off liquid; turn over squash in the baking dish so that it is cut side up. Drizzle with melted butter or margarine and sprinkle with Parmesan cheese, oregano, and parsley. Continue baking about 20 minutes or until tender, crusty and browned.

Submitted by Mary Beck, SSND from Mount Calvary, WI

118

Zucchini Rounds

Serves 4

⅓ **cup Bisquick**
¼ **cup Parmesan cheese**
2 eggs, beaten
½ **cup onions,** finely chopped
2 cups zucchini, shredded
Garlic powder and pepper, dash of each
Butter or margarine

Mix all ingredients together. In a frying pan heat a small amount of butter or margarine and spoon in small amounts of mixture. Turn as you would pancakes.

119

Alternative:

Spoon small clumps of mixture onto a lightly greased cookie sheet and bake at 350 degrees until golden brown. Turn once.

Submitted by Francette Malecha, SSND from Cambridge, MN

EMBRACING the VARIETY of
Seasonal Eating

strawberries • broccoli • lettuce • rhubarb • asparagus

Spring

SPRING is a time of purification, healing and rejuvenation. It is the season for a period of cleansing or fasting. *Lent is set in springtime.* In nature, the greens are growing freely, and these chlorophyll-rich foods are the body's best cleansers.

mushrooms • spinach• leeks• chives • green onions

120

blueberries • tomatoes • melons • peaches • corn • okra

Summer

The warmth of **SUMMER** requires a lighter diet and fresher, higher-water-content foods. And those are exactly the foods that nature provides during this season: succulent fruits and vegetables that are perfect for raw salads.

collards • cucumbers • eggplant • peppers • cabbage

pumpkins • pears • turnips • rutabagas • cranberries

Autumn

AUTUMN brings a big shift in energy, climate and diet. The harvest time provides us with an abundance of nourishing foods, including hardier root vegetables and squashes, as well as whole grains, legumes, seeds and nuts. As the weather cools, the diet can shift to foods with richer proteins and fats.

grapes •celery• persimmons • raspberries • kohlrabi

parsnips • sweet potatoes • onions • carrots • beets

Winter

121

In **WINTER,** we crave warming and sustaining foods. As in autumn, the mainstays of the diet are the complex carbohydrates found

in whole grains, squashes and root vegetables such as carrots, beets, potatoes, onions and garlic. This is the season for including dairy foods and meats, but they should never dominate the diet. More fish and high-mineral seaweeds are good in the winter, as is poultry. Winter fruits, like citrus, are high in the vitamin C we need to boost immunity.

November Evening

by Maura Eichner, SSND

On the barberry bush the ripe fruit hangs
in hazardous suspense of wind and cold;
the yellow of the walnut tree
in some dim memory of spattered gold.
Enough for the gum tree—a runner spent
and silent from the chase—
it leans against the oak, with all its breath
spilt out in scarlet pools about its base.
A day or two the maple will be done
with crimson noons and dusks of Chinese red;
by hours now the end of autumn slips away.
With silhouettes alone the eye is winter fed.

Tonight, ankle deep in great oak leaves,
mocha and russet, fawn and brown,
vaguely moist and still from somber rains,
we crush the seasoned harvest down.

Press the acorn underfoot, press the pod to earth,
knowing if this be death, this, too, is birth.

ENTREES

123

from Mother Caroline's pen:

Of the stores in New Orleans she wrote:

In April many kinds of fruit were already ripe: cranberries, strawberries, raspberries, blackberries, currants, gooseberries large as walnuts, sweet and aromatic; water or sugar melons; sweet and sour cherries, plums; early apples and pears. Besides these, oranges, citron, figs, coconuts, bananas and pineapples from Cuba can be had all year round. Then, too, tasty fish, crabs and oysters, and a great deal of fowl and animals from the southern forests.

The Letters of Mother Caroline Friess, School Sisters of Notre Dame, edited by Barbara Brumleve, SSND, p.77

125

Apple Meat Loaf

Serves 4

1 pound ground beef
1 small onion, diced
3 tablespoons apple, chopped
¼ teaspoon salt
¼ teaspoon pepper
¼ cup ketchup
1 teaspoon brown sugar

Preheat oven to 300 degrees. In a bowl, mix meat with onion, apple, salt, pepper, and ketchup. Add brown sugar. Put into a loaf pan and pour the sauce over it. Bake for 30 minutes.

Meat Loaf Sauce:
2 tablespoons margarine
2 tablespoons brown sugar
½ teaspoon dry mustard
½ cup ketchup
1 teaspoon Worcestershire sauce

Melt margarine and add the rest of the ingredients. Mix and pour over meat loaf before baking.

Submitted by Tessie Markus, SSND from Belleville, IL

School Sisters of Notre Dame
Celebrating **175** *years*

Aunt Lu's Cabbage Casserole

Serves 6

1 small head cabbage
1½ pounds ground beef
1 cup onion, chopped
¾ cups rice, uncooked
1 teaspoon salt
¼ teaspoon pepper
1 (10-ounce) can tomato soup
1 (8-ounce) can tomato sauce
1¾ cups water

127

Chop cabbage into medium pieces. Spread in the bottom of a 9x13 inch baking dish. Brown meat in a skillet, breaking up meat as it cooks. Add onions and cook until they are soft. Drain off the fat. Stir in rice, salt and pepper. Spoon mixture over cabbage.

In saucepan, heat soup, tomato sauce and water. Pour soup mixture over the mixture in baking dish. Cover tightly with aluminum foil and bake in a preheated 350 degree oven for 1½ hours. Fluff lightly with fork before serving.

Submitted by Jean Paul Zagorski, SSND from Milwaukee, WI

Baked Italian Inspiration

Serves 6

6 ounces large seashell macaroni
1 pound ground turkey
2 tablespoons oil
Salt
Garlic powder
4 ounces cream cheese
Parmesan cheese, grated, divided
4 ounces mozzarella cheese, grated, divided
16 ounces tomato sauce

128

Prepare seashell macaroni following directions on package. Fry ground turkey in oil. Salt to taste. Sprinkle with garlic powder. Remove from heat and allow to cool slightly before adding the cream cheese. Stir constantly until cheese melts and coats the turkey burger.

Place seashell macaroni in a 9x13 inch glass baking dish. Sprinkle with Parmesan cheese and half of the mozzarella cheese. Spread meat mixture on top of the cheese. Next, cover the meat with tomato sauce. Finally, cover with the remaining mozzarella cheese and sprinkle Parmesan cheese over all. Cover. Bake in a 325 degree oven for 30 minutes.

Submitted in 1993 by Mariel Kreuziger, SSND from Coolville, OH

Kenya

Beef and Mokimo (Nyama Na Mokimo)
....

Serves 6

This recipe is from the Kikuyu and Kamba tribes of Kenya. It would be made for a Sunday meal. Children will frequently take the leftover mokimo to school for lunch. It becomes stiff and they wrap it in paper to carry it.

The Mokimo:
6 medium potatoes
Salt and pepper, to taste
2 cups peas
2 cups water
2 cups corn or maize

129

Cut the potatoes, then boil and mash them. Combine peas with water and cook until ready to be mashed. Blend the mashed peas into the mashed potatoes until a smooth green color results. Cook the corn or maize. Fold in the kernel corn. The consistency should be that of firm mashed potatoes.

The Beef:
3 pounds beef
6 tablespoons flour
Margarine
3 cups white onions, cut up
2 cups water
Salt and pepper
Tabasco sauce or red pepper flakes

(continued on next page)

School Sisters of Notre Dame
Celebrating **175** *years*

Cut meat into small pieces. Roll the pieces in flour. In a large skillet, sauté the meat in margarine until lightly browned. Remove from skillet.

To the liquid in the skillet, blend in flour to make a roux (thickener). Add the cut up white onions and water stirring constantly until it is a smooth sauce. Return beef to skillet. Simmer until tender. Salt and pepper to taste. A little tabasco sauce or red pepper flakes may be added.

To serve, place a large mound of mokimo in the center of a dinner plate. Form a hole in the center about 2 inches in diameter. Fill the hole with ½ cup of sautéed beef and gravy.

Submitted by Janet Carne, SSND from Nairobi, Kenya

130

Beef Stew

Serves 10-12

6 tablespoons shortening
3 pounds beef, cubed
3 medium onions, chopped
1 cup red wine
4 cups water
2 beef bouillon cubes
1 clove garlic, chopped
2 tablespoons parsley, chopped
1 bay leaf
⅛ teaspoon thyme
1½ teaspoons salt
¼ teaspoon pepper
2 medium potatoes, quartered
5 medium carrots, cut in chunks
10 small white onions
4 stalks celery, cut in chunks
2 medium green peppers, cut in chunks
2 medium tomatoes, quartered

131

Over medium heat melt shortening in Dutch oven; add meat and brown well. Remove meat and set aside. Sauté chopped onions in Dutch oven until tender. Add meat, wine, water, bouillon, garlic, parsley, bay leaf, thyme, salt and pepper. Cover and simmer 1½ hours.

Add potatoes, carrots, white onions and celery. Cook 1 more hour, then add peppers and tomatoes. (Some cooks prefer to add the potatoes at this time.)

(continued on next page)

School Sisters of Notre Dame
Celebrating **175** *years*

If thicker gravy is desired add ½ cup flour to ¼ cup cold water; blend well. Add to stew and stir until stew boils and thickens.

Submitted by Betty Sweeney, SSND Associate from Baltimore, MD

10 Basic Principles

for Being in Right Relationship with the Land:

1. The land is God's.
2. People are God's stewards on the land.
3. The land's benefits are for everyone.
4. The land should be distributed equitably.
5. The land should be conserved and restored.
6. Land use planning must consider social and environmental impacts.
7. Land use should be appropriate to land quality.
8. The land should provide a moderate livelihood.
9. The land's workers should be able to become the land's owners.
10. The land's mineral wealth should be shared.

"Strangers and Guests: Toward Community in the Heartland"
Midwest Catholic Bishops (1980)

School Sisters *of* Notre Dame
Celebrating **175** *years*

Benachin

....

Serves 12

The Gambia's main dish. In The Gambia, people enjoy sitting in small groups and sharing from a common bowl of food. "Bena-chin" literally means "one pot." That's all you will need for this recipe – make sure it's a big one.

1 pound (½ kg) fish/meat/shrimp
2 tablespoons vinegar
2 tablespoons mustard
½ teaspoon black pepper
2 cloves garlic
2 jumbo cubes (bouillon cubes)
Salt to taste
2 cups oil
3 onions
10 tomatoes
¼ teaspoon hot pepper
1 medium eggplant, sliced
1 head cabbage, sliced
4 bitter tomatoes, sliced
1 small cassava, cut up
4 bay leaves
3 medium carrots, cut up
3 medium sweet potatoes or Irish potatoes, cut up
5 cups rice, uncooked
1 small can tomato paste (optional)

133

Marinate fish/meat with a little vinegar, mustard, pepper, one garlic clove, one jumbo cube and salt. Let sit in the refrigerator,

(continued on next page)

School Sisters *of* Notre Dame
Celebrating **175** *years*

covered, for about a half hour. In the oil, deep fry fish/meat and remove from pan when done.

Fry onions and tomatoes in the same pan and add the remaining garlic, hot pepper, black pepper and salt. When fried add 1 cup water. Allow it to boil for about 5 minutes, then put back the fried meat/fish and add eggplant, cabbage, bitter tomato, cassava, ba leaves, carrots, potatoes. Add more water as needed. Add secon jumbo cube and salt to taste. Boil until cooked. Remove all the vegetables and fish/meat.

Check the remaining sauce and add water to make 10 cups. Add salt to taste. Bring it to a boil, then put in cleaned rice. Allow it to cook and serve with the vegetables and meat/fish.

Note: *If you prefer white benachin, you use tomatoes only. If you li red benachin, you add both tomatoes and tomato paste.*

134   Submitted by the Sisters of The Gambia

O **TASTE** and **SEE**
THAT THE LORD IS GOOD.   Ps. 34:8a

School Sisters of Notre Dame
Celebrating **175** *years*

Black Bean Bake

Serves 6

2 cups rice, cooked
1 (15-ounce) can black beans, rinsed and drained
1 cup tomatoes, chopped
⅔ cup green onions, chopped
1 small can ripe olives, drained and sliced
1 cup salsa
½ teaspoon ground cumin
1½ cups cheese, shredded
2 cups tortilla chips, crushed

135

In an 8 inch baking dish, which has been coated with non-stick spray, layer:
Rice
Beans
Tomatoes
Onions
Olives
Salsa
Cumin
Cheese

Bake at 350 degrees for 20 minutes or until bubbly. Top with tortilla chips before serving.

Submitted by Nancy Traeger, SSND from Elm Grove, WI

Brunch Casserole

Serves 8

6 slices bread, cut into cubes
3 cups mild cheddar cheese, grated
1 cup cooked ham, cubed
¼ cup green pepper, chopped
½ cup onion, chopped

Combine above ingredients. Place in a greased 9X13 inch baking dish.

136

Sauce:
6 eggs
3 cups skim milk

Whisk together and pour over the ingredients in the baking dish. Refrigerate overnight or freeze for later use. If frozen, thaw before baking. Bake at 375 degrees for 45 minutes.

Submitted by Joan Bartosh, SSND from Rochester, MN

Busy Day Stew

Serves 10

2 pounds stew meat
1 cup turnip, cut in chunks
1 cup celery, diced
4 medium carrots, sliced
4 potatoes, cubed
1 cup onion, sliced
½ cup green pepper, chopped
1 (20-ounce) can tomatoes
1 teaspoon celery salt
1 package onion soup mix
½ cup minute tapioca
½ cup consommé
½ cup wine (optional)

137

Mix together all ingredients in a small roaster and bake in a slow
oven (300 degrees) for 4-5 hours. Do not brown the meat first.
Excellent taste, tender meat and thick sauce all in one package.
Enjoy.

Submitted by Dianne Poitras, SSND Associate from Regina, Saskatchewan,
Canada

School Sisters of Notre Dame
Celebrating **175** *years*

Charlie's Macaroni

Serves 8

This recipe was handed down from my grandmother who got it from Charles Mattani, an Italian building contractor in Fergus, Ontario, with whom my grandparents and their first four children lived for a few years during the depression. Charlie had a big house, a big garden and a heart of gold. The macaroni became a symbol of caring in our family. Once when mom was in the hospital, grandma brought a big pot of Charlie's macaroni over for supper. It was a treat. No one makes it as well as grandma even though she showed us the secret: fry the onions, butter and bacon until the froth is the right color: gold.

138

4-5 cups macaroni, uncooked
½ cup butter or olive oil
2 onions, chopped
8 slices bacon, cut up
1 small can tomato paste
2 cups tomatoes, diced
3-4 tablespoons cheddar cheese, shredded

Cook macaroni as directed. In a frying pan over medium heat, melt butter, add onions and sauté for 3-4 minutes; add bacon. Keep cooking until the froth is gold, not white and not brown. Add tomato paste, tomatoes and let simmer until macaroni is done. Stir into macaroni, add cheese and serve.

Submitted by Pat Stortz, SSND Associate from Waterdown, Ontario, Canada

Chicken and Dumplings

Serves 6

Our moms both made this when we were under the weather or just needed something to warm our innards. Marilyn's mom often sent her with this dish to friends and neighbors who had a death or illness in the family.

Cook and debone a whole chicken.
Cut into small pieces and place in broth from cooking.

For dumplings:
2 cups flour (can use whole wheat)
1 tablespoon shortening
1 teaspoon baking powder
¼ teaspoon salt
1 egg
¾ cup skim milk

139

Combine first four ingredients until mixture is crumbly. Add egg and milk. Roll out and cut in ½ inch squares. Place in hot broth and cook for about 10 minutes, or until dumplings are done.

Submitted by Marilyn Wussler, SSND and Charlene Zeisset, SSND from St. Louis, MO

Chicken Casserole

Serves 6-8

4 cups chicken chunks, cooked
2 tablespoons lemon juice
¾ cup mayonnaise
1 teaspoon salt
2 cups celery, chopped
4 hard boiled eggs, sliced
1 teaspoon onion, minced
¾ cup cream of mushroom soup
2 teaspoons pimentos
1 cup cheese, grated
1½ cups crushed potato chips (baked chips, if possible)
⅔ cup almonds, finely chopped

140

Combine all except cheese, chips and nuts. Place in a casserole dish. Cover. Refrigerate overnight. Top with cheese, chips and nuts. Bake at 400 degrees for 20-25 minutes.

Submitted by Tessie Markus, SSND from Belleville, IL

follow the **LOAF** *principles*

Locally   **O**rganically   **A**nimal   **F**airly
produced   grown   friendly   traded

NOURISHMENT FOR THE WHOLE EARTH

School Sisters of Notre Dame
Celebrating **175** *years*

Chicken Jerusalem

Serves 8

Because I lived with my mother who did all the cooking, after her death I was at a loss for many reasons about what to do in a kitchen. However, a young nephew came to my rescue by giving me a copy of Peg Bracken's "I Hate to Cook." With that as my support, the first time I held a dinner party I had 25 guests including 2 bishops and about 8 other clergy. Apparently I had more nerve than good sense because I had never tried the recipe before that evening. Amazingly, it was a big hit.

141

3 pounds chicken pieces
1½ teaspoons salt
¼ teaspoon pepper
½ teaspoon paprika
6 tablespoons butter or margarine, divided
¼ pound mushrooms, cut in large pieces
2 tablespoons flour
⅔ cup chicken consommé or bouillon
2 tablespoons sherry or other red wine
1 can artichoke hearts

Season chicken with salt, pepper and paprika. Brown it in four tablespoons of butter or margarine. Place in large casserole. Sauté mushrooms in remaining butter or margarine and sprinkle with flour. Add chicken consommé and wine. Stir. Arrange artichoke hearts among chicken pieces; pour sauce over them. Bake covered at 350 degrees for 30-45 minutes.

Submitted by Betty Sweeney, SSND Associate from Baltimore, MD

School Sisters of Notre Dame
Celebrating **175** *years*

Chicken Lasagna

Serves 8

½ **cup margarine**
½ **cup flour**
½ **teaspoon salt**
½ **teaspoon basil**
3 cups chicken broth
2½ cups chicken, cooked and diced
1 pound cottage cheese, low fat
1 egg, slightly beaten
½ **pound lasagna noodles,** cooked or uncooked
½ **pound mozzarella cheese,** sliced
Parmesan cheese, grated
10-ounce package frozen spinach (optional)

Melt margarine. Blend in flour, salt and basil. Stir in broth. Cook until mixture thickens and comes to a boil. Add chicken. In a separate bowl, mix together cottage cheese with egg. Grease 9x13 inch pan. Place ⅓ chicken mix into pan. Top with ½ noodles, ½ cottage cheese mixture and ½ mozzarella. Repeat. End with remaining chicken mixture. Top with Parmesan cheese. Bake in 375 degree oven for approximately 45 minutes until bubbling. Let stand 15-20 minutes before serving. For color, defrost 1 package of frozen spinach, squeeze out water and spread between layers.

Submitted by Georganne Pearson, SSND from Dover, NH

Chicken Pot Pie
....

Serves 6

¼ **cup butter or margarine**
1½ **cups celery,** chopped
2 **cups carrots,** sliced
1 **cup onions,** chopped
¼ **cup flour**
1¾ **cups chicken broth**
3 **cups chicken or turkey,** cooked and cut up
½ **cup half & half or 2% milk**
¼ **cup parsley,** chopped
½ **teaspoon poultry seasoning**
⅛ **teaspoon pepper**
½ **teaspoon salt**

Preheat oven to 425 degrees.
In a 4 quart saucepan, over medium heat sauté celery, carrots and onions in butter or margarine until tender. Stir in flour until blended. Gradually stir in broth. Cook until mixture boils, stirring constantly. Add chicken, parsley, seasoning and milk. Stir well. Spoon or pour mixture into 12x8 inch baking dish. Cover with crust. Bake 25 minutes or until golden brown.

Crust:
1 **cup flour**
¼ **teaspoon salt**
½ **teaspoon baking powder**
⅓ **cup margarine**
Egg (yolk only)
1-2 **tablespoons cold water**

(continued on next page)

*School Sisters of **Notre Dame***
Celebrating **175** *years*

With pastry blender or fork cut in flour, salt, baking powder and margarine, until mixture resembles small crumbs. Stir in egg yolk.

Add cold water mixing lightly with fork until pastry just holds together. With hands shape into ball. On slightly floured surface roll pastry into 14x10 inch rectangle or shape of pan. Cut slashes or design in center. Place loosely over filling. Trim edge leaving 1 inch overhang. Fold it over. Make high-standing fluted edge.
Regular pie pastry can be used in place of the above crust.

Submitted by Sharon Rempe, SSND from St. Louis, MO

....

Chicken

144

ORGANIC *chickens are fed a diet with no additives, not treated with antibiotics and raised under specific humane conditions. These are USDA requirements.*

NATURAL *chickens contain no artificial ingredients or added color. But unless the label reads "no antibiotics," there's no guarantee that there aren't any.*

FREE RANGE *chickens are allowed some room to roam outside the coop—but how much roam isn't regulated. Some, but not all, free range chickens are raised on a natural diet.*

Chicken Schnitzel

Serving equal to number of breasts.

This "Schnitzel" dinner accompanied by potatoes, veggies and salad is a must for our family for Christmas Eve. They request it also for birthdays and Thanksgiving.

Chicken breasts, boneless
Flour
Bread crumbs
2 eggs
Milk
Salt to taste
Olive oil

145

Put flour and bread crumbs onto two separate plates. Crack eggs into bowl, add a little milk and mix till fluffy. Add salt according to taste. Cover each chicken breast with flour, dunk into egg mixture and then roll in bread crumbs. Fry in olive oil (both sides) until golden brown. Then place in oven, uncovered, to bake at 325 degrees for one half hour.

Submitted by Hermie Schuster, SSND Associate from Kitchener, Ontario, Canada

Chili (Vegetarian)

Serves 4-6

2 tablespoons olive oil
1 large green or red pepper, chopped
2 large onions, chopped
2 (16 ounce) cans kidney or red beans (1 more can
for thicker chili)
2 (16 ounce) cans crushed tomatoes
5-6 ounces ketchup
1 (12-ounce) can beer
2 tablespoons brown sugar
2 tablespoons Worcestershire sauce
3-4 tablespoons chili powder, or to taste

Sauté pepper and onions in olive oil until tender. Add remaining ingredients and bring to a boil. Then simmer, covered, for about 30 minutes.

Submitted by Paulette Zimmerman, SSND from St. Louis, MO

146

Creamy Baked Chicken Breast

Serves 6-8

4 whole chicken breasts, split
8 slices Swiss cheese
1 (10.75-ounce) can condensed cream of chicken soup
¼ cup milk
1 cup herb-seasoned stuffing mix, crushed
¼ cup margarine, melted

Arrange chicken in greased 9X13 inch pan. Top each piece with cheese slices. Combine soup and milk and spoon evenly over chicken. Sprinkle stuffing mix over chicken, drizzle melted margarine over crumbs. Bake at 350 degrees for 45-55 minutes.

147

Submitted by Sharon Rempe, SSND from St. Louis, MO

Eat mindfully. Savor your food.
Thich Nhat Hanh

School Sisters of Notre Dame
Celebrating **175** *years*

Curried Chicken

Serves 4

1 (10.75-ounce) can condensed cream of chicken soup
½ cup mayonnaise
¼ teaspoon curry powder
½ teaspoon lemon juice
Salt and pepper
1 (10-ounce) package broccoli, cooked, drained, chopped
2 cups chicken, cooked, chopped
Buttered bread crumbs

148

Combine soup, mayonnaise, curry powder, lemon juice, salt and pepper. Layer half of broccoli, chicken and soup mixture in greased 2-quart shallow casserole. Sprinkle with bread crumbs and repeat layers. Bake covered at 350 degrees for 30 minutes. Uncover for the last 10 minutes.

Submitted by Clared Coyne, SSND from Chatawa, MS

Domburi (A Big Bowl)

Serves 4

Domburi means a big bowl, larger than rice bowls. A big bowl of rice topped with cooked egg, mixed with meat and vegetables. Western soup bowls may be used. Serve with spoons. This dish is very simple and easy to prepare. This is served for lunch with fruit or waldorf salad or raw fruit for dessert.

400 grams (13 ounces) beef or pork, sliced as for sukiyaki
4 to 5 round onions, peeled and cut length-wise
1 bunch of greens, Japanese mitsuba (or greens such as spinach)
½ cup bamboo sprouts, if in season, or canned bamboo sprouts
1 package dried shiitake (or mushrooms), soaked in water for 10 minutes
½ cup soy sauce
¼ cup sugar
5 or 6 eggs, depending on size
Nori (edible seaweed)

149

Peel and slice onions. Cook in fat in one frying pan while meat is frying in another. When meat is browned, add the onions, and other ingredients (except eggs) to pan and cool for about 15 or 20 minutes.

The eggs are beaten lightly together and poured over the cooked mixture. The lid is replaced and the eggs are cooked until they have set (the eggs should be only half cooked). Ladle onto the rice in bowls. Pour in the remaining liquid, top with nori (edible seaweed), toasted and serve immediately.

Submitted by Janet Tanaka, SSND from Kyoto, Japan

School Sisters of Notre Dame
Celebrating **175** *years*

Easy Chicken Dish

Serves 4-8

4-8 chicken breasts, skinless
1 bottle (regular size) French dressing
1 package dry onion soup mix
1 (16-ounce) can whole cranberry sauce

Arrange chicken in greased baking dish. Mix together dressing, soup mix and cranberries. Pour over chicken breasts. Bake in a 350 degree oven for 35 minutes.

Submitted by Patricia Warnick, SSND from Baltimore, MD

150

Easy Chicken Recipe

Serves 6-8

6-8 chicken pieces
Cooking oil
Rice, uncooked
Onion, diced
Onion soup mix
Water, twice as much as the rice
Soy sauce (optional)

Sauté chicken pieces in oil and then remove from pan. Brown desired amount of rice and onion in the grease. Place chicken back into the frying pan. Add packet of onion soup mix, water, and a little soy sauce, if desired. Place lid on pan and simmer on low heat for about 30-40 minutes checking from time to time to see if there is enough liquid. Serve when chicken is done and the liquid on the rice has cooked down.

151

Submitted by Clared Coyne, SSND from Chatawa, MS

Fast And Tasty Chili

Serves 6-8

1-2 tablespoons olive oil
1 medium sweet onion, diced
1 pound lean ground beef
1 pound can tomatoes, diced
1 pound can tomato sauce
1 pound can red kidney beans, rinsed and drained
1 (6-ounce) can tomato paste plus 6-ounces of water
2 tablespoons chili powder
1 teaspoon black pepper
4 cups water
2 cups rice, uncooked

152

Heat olive oil in large skillet. Brown onion. Add ground beef and thoroughly brown. Drain off any grease and set aside. In a large pot or crock-pot add the diced tomatoes, tomato sauce, kidney beans, tomato paste plus water, chili powder and black pepper. Stir the meat mixture into the tomato and bean mixture. Cook on medium heat until just before boiling. Simmer until ready to serve. If using a crock-pot, cook on low heat about 2 hours or until ready to serve.

In a saucepan, boil the 4 cups water, add the rice. Reduce heat, cover and simmer for about 15 minutes, until the rice is fluffy. For best results, do not remove lid. Serve chili over rice.

Submitted by Yvonne Conley, SSND from Milwaukee, WI

Five-Minute Sweet and Sour Stir Fry

Serves 4

2 tablespoons oil
1 medium onion, coarsely chopped
1 red pepper, cut in long, thin slices
½ green pepper, cut in long, thin slices
1 pound firm tofu, cut into bite-sized pieces
Salt, to taste
Pepper, to taste
1 (16-ounce) jar sweet and sour sauce

In nonstick pan, heat oil. Stir fry onions and peppers for 2 minutes. Add tofu and fry for 1 minute. Sprinkle with salt and pepper. Fold in sauce. Reduce heat to medium and cook until heated through. Serve over rice or Chinese noodles.

153

Submitted by Suzanne Moynihan, SSND from Mount Calvary, WI

Golden Glow Pork Chops

Serves 5-6

5-6 pork chops
Salt and pepper
1 (29-ounce) can cling peach halves, save ¼ cup syrup from peaches
¼ cup brown sugar
½ teaspoon cinnamon
¼ teaspoon ground cloves
1 (8-ounce) can tomato sauce
¼ cup vinegar

154

Lightly brown pork chops on both sides in a large skillet or a slow cooker with browning unit. Pour off excess fat. Sprinkle chops with salt and pepper. Arrange chops in slow cooker. Place drained peach halves on top. Combine brown sugar, cinnamon, cloves, tomato sauce, ¼ cup syrup from peaches, and vinegar. Pour tomato mixture over all. Cover and cook on low for 4 to 6 hours.

Submitted by Marie Regine Redig, SSND and Gladys Marie Courtade, SSND from Milwaukee, WI

Goulash

Serves 2

¼ pound ground beef
1 small onion, diced
¼ teaspoon salt
⅛ teaspoon pepper
¾ cup tomato juice
⅓ cup elbow macaroni, uncooked
⅓ cup water

Break up meat in a 20-ounce microwave-safe casserole. Add onion. Microwave on high about 2 minutes or until meat is no longer pink. Break up the meat and drain. Add salt, pepper, tomato juice, macaroni and water. Cover with plastic wrap with a few holes poked into it. Microwave on high for about 10 minutes or until macaroni is tender. Stir once during microwaving.

155

Submitted in 1992 by Joan Bartosh, SSND from Rochester, MN

School Sisters of Notre Dame
Celebrating **175** *years*

Hamburger Casserole

Serves 6

1 pound ground beef
1 onion, chopped
1 (10.75-ounce) can condensed cream of mushroom soup
Cheese, grated, to taste
Tater tots

In a skillet, fry the ground beef with the onion. Drain. Mix with mushroom soup. Add as much grated cheese as you like. Place in 2-quart casserole. Cover with tater tots. Bake at 350 degrees about 45 minutes or until potatoes are brown.

156

Submitted by Tessie Markus, SSND from Belleville, IL

Inside Out Ravioli

Serves 6

1 (10-ounce) package frozen spinach (1¼ cups), chopped
1 tablespoon oil
1 pound ground beef
1 medium onion, chopped
1 clove garlic, minced
1 (15-ounce) container spaghetti sauce w/mushrooms
1 (8-ounce) can tomato sauce
½ teaspoon salt
⅛ teaspoon pepper
2 cups elbow macaroni, cooked
1 cup cheddar cheese, shredded
½ cup bread crumbs, Italian style
2 eggs, well beaten
¼ cup salad oil

157

Preheat oven to 350 degrees. Cook spinach according to directions, drain and reserve liquid. Add water to make 1 cup liquid and set aside. Heat oil and sauté beef, onion and garlic. When browned, add spinach liquid, spaghetti sauce, tomato sauce, salt and pepper. Simmer uncovered 10 to 15 minutes. Combine spinach, macaroni, cheese, bread crumbs, eggs and salad oil. Pour into greased 9x13 inch pan. Top with sauce. Bake 30 minutes.

Submitted by Marie Torno, SSND from Chatawa, MS

School Sisters of Notre Dame
Celebrating **175** *years*

King Ranch Casserole

Serves 6-8

1 fryer chicken, cooked and deboned
or
2 pounds ground meat, browned and drained
1 package corn tortillas, cut into pieces
1 onion, chopped
2 cups Monterey Jack cheese, grated

Sauce:
1 (10.75-ounce) can condensed cream of mushroom soup
1 (10.75-ounce) can condensed cream of chicken soup
½ can tomatoes with green chilies
Broth from chicken, water or milk

158

Mix together the ingredients for the sauce. Blend until smooth. Into a 2½ quart casserole, place in layers half of the chicken or meat, half the package tortillas, half the onion, half the sauce and half the cheese. Repeat layers, ending with cheese. Bake, uncovered, at 350 degrees for 1 hour.

Submitted by Marie Torno, SSND from Chatawa, MS

Marinade for Pork Tenderloin

For 2 pounds of tenderloin:

2-3 cloves garlic, crushed
1 tablespoon balsamic vinegar
Juice of 2 limes
3 tablespoons brown sugar
¼ cup orange juice concentrate, or orange juice
¼ cup sesame seeds (optional)

Combine ingredients, pour over tenderloins and marinate in refrigerator for 2-4 hours. Remove tenderloins and discard marinade. Bake in a glass baking dish or pan in a 325 degree oven. Usually baking time is 45 minutes for one pound, so bake for 1½ hours.

159

Submittted by Gen Cassani, SSND from St Louis, MO

Mom's Sloppy Joe

Serves 6

1½ **pounds ground beef**
1 **small onion**, chopped
1 **(10.75-ounce) can condensed chicken gumbo soup**
1 **tablespoon mustard**
3 **tablespoons barbecue sauce**
1 **tablespoon sugar**

Put meat and onion in pan and brown the meat. Drain. Add the soup and other ingredients. When it begins to cook turn burner down and simmer for 1 hour and 15 minutes. Stir now and then so it does not stick to pan. Serve over buns.

160

Submitted by Joan Frey, SSND from Milwaukee, WI

Just four corporations control

more than 80 percent of the beef market

in the United States and about 60 percent

of the pork market.

National Catholic Rural Life Conference

School Sisters of Notre Dame
Celebrating **175** *years*

Nun Better Chicken

Serves 5

5 chicken breasts
1 package onion soup mix
1 can whole berries cranberry sauce
1 bottle Russian salad dressing
Prepared bread stuffing

Cut chicken breasts into chunks. Place in a 7X9 inch baking dish.
Sprinkle onion soup mix over chicken. Spread cranberries over
this. Pour on salad dressing.

Cook covered in 350 degree oven for one hour. Serve over bread
stuffing.

161

Submitted by John Vianney Zullo, SSND from Bridgeport, CT

Open-Faced Tacos

Serves 8

Bowl 1 **Nacho cheese chips**

Bowl 2 **1½ pounds ground beef**
Onion, chopped
2 cans red kidney beans, drained
1 large bottle Catalina-style French Dressing
Brown meat and onions together, drain, add kidney
beans and dressing. Heat through.

162

Bowl 3 **Cheddar cheese**, shredded
Bowl 4 **Lettuce**, shredded
Bowl 5 **Tomato** chunks
Bowl 6 **Onion**, chopped

Bottle mild taco sauce

Serve buffet style. Layer on plates beginning with chips and
following order through.

Submitted by Alice Giere, SSND from Elm Grove, WI

Orange Glazed Meatloaf

Serves 6

Great cold the next day for lunch.

2 pounds lean hamburger
1½ cups bread or cracker crumbs
1 egg
1 medium onion, cut up
Pepper and salt, to taste
½ cup orange juice
Juice of one lemon (about 1 tablespoon)
½ teaspoon dry mustard
6 tablespoons brown sugar
1 orange, sliced, peeled or unpeeled as you prefer

Mix all except last three items. In the bottom of a large loaf pan, sprinkle the brown sugar and mustard. Place a layer of orange slices over this. Press the meat mixture into the pan. Bake at 350 degrees for 1 hour. Let stand 10 minutes. Invert onto a serving platter and serve.

Submitted by Pat Stortz, SSND Associate from Waterdown, Ontario, Canada

Orange Raisin Sauce for Ham

Serves 6

¼ cup sugar
1 tablespoon corn starch
1 cup boiling water
Juice and rind of one orange
½ cup raisins
1 tablespoon margarine

Mix sugar and corn starch. Add boiling water and cook until clear. Add orange juice and rind, raisins and margarine. Cook until thick. Pour over ham before baking.

164

Submitted by Joan Bartosh, SSND from Rochestser, MN

" *Treat all living beings*
with respect and consideration: prevent cruelty to

animals kept in human societies and protect them

from suffering."   Earth Charter, Principle 15

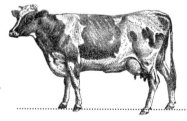

For more information on the Earth Charter www. earthcharter.org/

School Sisters of Notre Dame
Celebrating **175** *years*

Oven-Barbecued Chicken

Serves 6

1 chicken, cut into serving pieces
½ teaspoon salt
¼ teaspoon black pepper
⅓ cup water
½ cup ketchup
2 tablespoons brown sugar
¼ cup cider vinegar
1 tablespoon prepared spicy brown mustard
1 tablespoon Worcestershire sauce
¼ teaspoon dried red pepper, crushed

165

Put chicken into a greased 9x13 inch baking pan. Sprinkle with salt and pepper. In a small bowl, mix the water, ketchup, sugar, vinegar, mustard, Worcestershire sauce and red pepper. Pour mixture over the chicken. Bake uncovered at 400 degrees for 45 minutes. Before serving, tip the baking dish and skim fat from the sauce.

Variation:
Use thick pork chops instead of chicken.

Submitted by Nancy Traeger, SSND from Elm Grove, WI

School Sisters of Notre Dame
Celebrating **175** *years*

Pasta Tutto Maré

Serves 6

Pasta
2 cups chicken broth
½ cup butter or margarine
1 pound shrimp, shelled
½ pound lump crabmeat, drained
1 can clams, drained
Garlic powder, to taste
Salt and pepper, to taste
Parsley, chopped
Parmesan cheese

166

Cook your favorite pasta according to package directions. Form a base by heating broth and butter until butter is melted. Add seafood to broth and butter base. Heat until shrimp turns pink. Add garlic powder, salt and pepper to taste. Mix with pasta, garnish with parsley and Parmesan cheese, and serve.

Submitted by Marie Torno, SSND from Chatawa, MS

Pig Tails

One pig tail per person

These are always a hit when I bring them to our Associate potlucks. Pig tails are something of a delicacy among many people in this very German area of Ontario. However, the fat prevented some people from trying them. This is a much healthier variation.

Pig tails, one for each person
Brown sugar
Beef gravy

Trim excess fat off tails. Put into roasting pan, salt and bake at 350 degrees for about an hour or more depending on number of tails. Drain all fat off and pour "sauce" over them. Sauce is equal amounts brown sugar and beef gravy. Bake at slow heat, 300 degrees, for a long time, 1 to 2 to 3 hours, depending upon the quantity.

167

Submitted by Cleo Wagner, SSND Associate from Kitchener, Ontario, Canada

Pizza Fondue

Serves 4

½ **pound ground beef**
½ **onion or 1 teaspoon onion salt**
2 tablespoons butter or margarine
2 cans pizza sauce
2 tablespoons cornstarch
½ **teaspoon oregano**
¼ **teaspoon garlic salt**
10 ounces cheddar cheese, grated
French bread, cubed

Brown ground beef and onion in butter. Add pizza sauce.
Blend cornstarch, oregano and garlic salt together. Add this to
ground beef and pizza sauce. Add cheddar cheese by thirds, stir
until melted. Serve with French bread cubes.

Submitted by Marie Torno, SSND from Chatawa, MS

Pork Chops Supreme

Serving: 1 chop per person

Pork chops
Salt and pepper
Onion, sliced
Lemon, sliced
Ketchup
Brown sugar
Water

Salt and pepper chops. Brown in a little of their own fat. Place chops in an oblong baking dish. On top of each chop put a slice of onion, a slice of lemon and 1 tablespoon ketchup and then sprinkle a clump of brown sugar over this. Add up to ½ inch water in the dish along the side, not over the chops. Cover with foil and bake at 350 degrees for 1 hour.

169

Submitted by Joan Frey, SSND from Milwaukee, WI

School Sisters of Notre Dame
Celebrating **175** *years*

Portuguese Chicken

Serves 6

6-8 chicken pieces
1 (15-ounce) can tomatoes
Green pepper, sliced
Onion, diced
Parmesan cheese, grated

Sauté chicken in frying pan. Add tomatoes, green peppers, and onions. Place lid on pan and simmer on low heat for about 30-40 minutes. Check the liquid level from time to time. Add water if necessary. When done, top with cheese and serve.

170

Submitted by Clared Coyne, SSND from Chatawa, MS

Salmon Festive

Serves 6

Those of us who were blessed to be in the novitiate at Villa Assumption in the late 30s and early 40s will probably remember with fondness Sister Herman's special salmon dish. After much urging Sister gave us her recipe. She didn't give us the recipe for sauce. Perhaps she thought we knew how to make it.

1 package baking powder biscuit dough, prepared
Melted butter as needed
1 can red salmon
6 sweet pickles, diced
3 hard boiled eggs, diced
2 cups medium white sauce
½ pound American cheese, grated

171

Roll out 2 layers of biscuit dough to fit bread pan. Brush melted butter between layers. Bake in hot oven, 450 degrees, for 15 minutes.

Drain and flake salmon. Combine salmon, some pickles and eggs. Remove baked biscuit layers from oven. Separate layers; spread bottom layer generously with salmon mixture.

Combine white sauce and cheese; stir over heat until smooth. Pour sauce over biscuit layer and salmon; top with second biscuit layer. Pour over it the remaining sauce. Garnish with remaining pickles and egg slices.

(continued on next page)

School Sisters of Notre Dame
Celebrating **175** *years*

Standard white sauce:

4 tablespoons butter or margarine
4 tablespoons flour
2 cups milk

Melt butter, blend in flour until smooth. Add milk gradually stirring ur
the mixture begins to boil. Reduce heat and cook for another three
minutes.

Submitted by Betty Sweeney, SSND Associate from Baltimore, MD

Mother Caroline Friess, SSND
writes of her experience of
the streets of New York after
the Sisters arrival there on
July 31, 1847.

172

. . . American versions of animal and plant life in the markets and stores; tables heavily laden with fish lying in brine or countless crabs; wagons filled with oysters; watermelons and cantaloupes sold by the pound as the only relief on the hot summer days; also, coconut and pineapples, oranges, figs, almonds and dates . . .

so much for only a few cents!

The Letters of Mother Caroline Friess, School Sisters of Notre Dam
edited by Barbara Brumleve, SSND, p. 25.

School Sisters of Notre Dame
Celebrating **175** *years*

Salmon on Sautéed Greens

Serves 4

In our parish of 25,000 new Canadians, we have a network for eco-friendly living. We buy locally, eat organic and use toxic-free house cleaners. We are Immigrants to Canada and we choose to live this way because we value the land and we want a future for our children.

4 tablespoons extra virgin olive oil
4 boneless salmon fillets, about 5-ounces each
½ pound greens (spinach, mustard greens, etc.)
Tamari sauce
½ cup onion, chopped
4 cloves garlic, minced
2 teaspoons fresh ginger, minced
3 ripe tomatoes, cut in pieces
2 tablespoons fresh parsley, chopped

173

Spoon 1 tablespoon olive oil over salmon fillet. Cover and refrigerate. In a skillet, heat 1 tablespoon of remaining olive oil and sauté the greens for 1 minute. Mix in 1 teaspoon Tamari sauce. Pour on a plate and set aside. Heat remaining 2 tablespoons olive oil in skillet and sauté the onion for 1 minute, then the garlic and ginger for another minute. Add the tomatoes, 1 teaspoon Tamari sauce and cook for 2 minutes. Broil Salmon fillet 4-6 minutes on each side. Do not over cook. Spoon the tomato mixture over the greens on plate and top with salmon. Sprinkle parsley on salmon and serve.

Submitted by Celeste Reinhart, SSND from Toronto, Ontario, Canada

School Sisters of Notre Dame
Celebrating **175** *years*

Salmon

Overfishing,

formally defined as "situations where one or more fish stocks are reduced below pre-defined levels of acceptance by fishing activities, means that fish stocks are depleted to the point where they may not be able to recover. In areas such as the eastern coast of Canada and the northeastern coast of the U.S., certain species have been fished to collapse, which consequently caused the fishing communities that relied on those stocks to collapse.

In some cases, depleted fish stocks have been restored; however, this is only possible when the species' ecosystem remains intact. If the species depletion causes an imbalance in the ecosystem, not only is it difficult for the depleted stocks to return to sustainable levels, other species dependent on the depleted stocks may become imbalanced, causing further problems.

174

ECO-BEST

Anchovies
Char, Arctic (farmed)
Mackerel, Atlantic
Mussels
Oysters (farmed)
Sablefish (Alaska, Canada)
Salmon, wild (Alaska)
Sardines
Trout, rainbow (farmed)
Tuna, albacore (U.S., Canada)

ECO-OK

Clams (wild)
Cod, Pacific (trawl)
Crab, snow/tanner
Flounder/sole (Pacific)
Lobster, American/Maine
Scallop, sea (N.E., Canada)
Shrimp (U.S. wild)
Squid
Tilapia (Latin America)
Tuna, canned light

ECO-WORST

Chilean sea bass
Grouper
Monkfish
Orange roughy
Salmon, farmed/Atlantic
Shark
Swordfish (imported)
Tilefish (Gulf of Mexico/South Atlan
Tuna, bigeye/yellowfin
(imported longline)
Tuna, bluefin

Environmental Defense Fund
http://www.edf.org

San Antonio Chili

Serves 12

3 pounds meat, coarsely ground
6 tablespoons chili powder
1 tablespoon oregano
1 tablespoon cumin
1 tablespoon salt
½ tablespoon cayenne pepper
2 large cloves garlic, minced
1 teaspoon Tabasco sauce
1½ quarts water
¼ cup white cornmeal

In Dutch oven, brown ground meat; drain. Add seasoning
and water; heat to boil. Reduce heat, cover and simmer for
1 hour and 30 minutes. Skim off fat. Stir in cornmeal and simmer
uncovered for 30 minutes. Stir occasionally.

Submitted by Marie Torno, SSND from Chatawa, MS

175

There is no such thing
as a little garlic.
Anonymous

Garlic

School Sisters *of* Notre Dame
Celebrating **175** *years*

Sauerkraut Hot Dish

Serves 4

My mother's recipe that I love to make.

1 pound hamburger
Salt and pepper, to taste
Onion, chopped
1 quart sauerkraut
1 can condensed cream of chicken or mushroom soup
½ soup can water
1 cup noodles, uncooked

176

Brown hamburger with salt, pepper and onion. Drain off fat. Drain sauerkraut and add to hamburger along with soup. Add water and uncooked noodles. Put in casserole and bake at 350 degrees for 1 hour.

Submitted by Bernelle Taube, SSND from Northfield, MN

COOKING *A Celebration of*
EARTH'S GIFTS

Second to None Turkey Casserole

Serves 8-10

2 tablespoons olive oil
1 medium onion, chopped
2 stalks celery, chopped
½ cup green pepper, chopped
½ cup red pepper, chopped
Fresh ground pepper, to taste
1 can cream of mushroom soup and 1 soup can milk
½ can cream of chicken soup
1 (7-ounce) package macaroni rings
1 pound medium size egg noodles
1 can mushrooms, drained
1 (5-ounce) can water chestnuts, drained
4 cups broccoli, cooked
4 cups turkey, cooked
½ cup bread crumbs

177

Mix together all ingredients except bread crumbs and place in casserole dish. Sprinkle bread crumbs on top. Bake at 325 degrees for 30 minutes.

Submitted by Mary Eric Militzer, SSND and Aloyse Hessburg, SSND from Milwaukee, WI

School Sisters of Notre Dame
Celebrating **175** *years*

Seven Layer Hot Dish

Serves 4

4 potatoes, sliced
4 carrots, sliced
1 onion, sliced
¼ cup rice, uncooked
1 can peas, with juice
1 can condensed tomato soup
1 pound ground beef
1 cup water
Season to taste

178

In a casserole dish, layer ingredients in order listed. Bake uncovered in a 350 degree oven for 1¼ to 2 hours.

Submitted by Rita Mary Schweihs, SSND from Homer Glen, IL

Shrimp a la Crème

Serves 4

This recipe appeared in a cookbook put together by the 1901 class of the Academy of Our Lady (A.O.L.) in 1925 to raise money for the chapel.

Cream Sauce:
2 tablespoons butter
2 tablespoons flour
1½ cups milk

Melt butter in saucepan over low heat. Blend in flour, stirring until mixture is smooth and bubbly. Remove from heat. Stir in milk. Heat to boiling, stirring constantly. Boil and stir for one minute.

179

1 cup shrimp, chopped
1 cup peas
⅛ teaspoon paprika
1 teaspoon salt
1 teaspoon parsley, chopped
½ teaspoon beef extract
1 teaspoon lemon juice
1 egg yolk
¼ teaspoon mustard

Mix together and add to cream sauce. Heat through.

Submitted by M. Charissia Powers, SSND (deceased)

School Sisters of Notre Dame
Celebrating **175** *years*

Shrimp or Crawfish Etoufee (Cajun Stew)

Serves 4-6

½ cup (1 stick) butter or margarine
3 stalks celery, diced
1 medium onion, diced
1 green pepper, diced
2 or 3 cloves garlic, chopped fine
1 teaspoon Italian seasoning
1 teaspoon parsley flakes
1 can Ro-tel tomatoes with green chilies
1 can condensed cream of mushroom soup, undiluted
1 small can V-8 juice
Dash of Worcestershire sauce
1 good "slug" sherry wine
1 to 1½ pounds shrimp or crawfish, cleaned and boiled
Salt and pepper, to taste
Cooked rice

In large saucepan, melt butter and sauté celery, onion, pepper and garlic. Add spices, tomatoes and soup. Stir well and then gradually stir in V-8 juice. Add Worcestershire sauce and sherry and simmer 15-30 minutes, stirring occasionally. If it gets too thick, add more V-8 juice. It should be the consistency of gravy. Add shrimp or crawfish and heat 10 more minutes. Salt and pepper to taste. Serve over rice.

Submitted by Ruth Speh, SSND from St. Louis, MO (deceased)

Spaghetti Sauce

Makes 4-5 quarts One quart serves 4-6 people

These vegetables and herbs, except for the celery and garlic, are grown in my garden.

12-15 pounds tomatoes
1 medium-sized zucchini, cubed
1 medium-sized eggplant, cubed
1 cup green pepper, cut up
1 cup celery, cut up
2 cups onion, chopped

181

Blanch tomatoes by scalding in boiling water. Put in cold water and then peel, and cut in halves or quarters. Put tomatoes in pot. Add zucchini and eggplant, green pepper and celery. Cook. As the vegetables cook, ladle off the juice until the sauce thickens, about 1-2 hours. Add the onions. Then add the following seasonings:

2 tablespoons brown sugar
1 tablespoon parsley
1 tablespoon oregano
½ teaspoon pepper
2 garlic cloves, minced
1 tablespoon basil
1½ tablespoons canning salt
1 jalapeno pepper, seeded and chopped

(continued on next page)

Cook until sauce becomes slightly thicker, about 15 minutes to ½ ho
Makes about 4-5 quarts. Fill jars and seal. Process 45 minutes in boili
water. This sauce can be used as salsa with some melted cheese, f
hot dishes or for pizza.

Submitted by Gloria Degele, SSND from St. Paul, MN

THE NUTRITION FACTS AND INGREDIENT LABELS

These labels give us the information we need to make informed
food choices and compare products. Consumer interests,
health needs, and expanding scientific knowledge on the role
food plays in health and disease all contribute to the content
and look of the Nutrition Facts table.

DID YOU KNOW THAT

* a healthy diet low in sodium and high in potassium may
  reduce the risk of high blood pressure;
* a healthy diet adequate in calcium and vitamin D may
  reduce the risk of osteoporosis;
* a healthy diet low in saturated fat and trans fat may reduce
  the risk of heart disease;
* a healthy diet rich in vegetables and fruit may reduce the
  risk of some types of cancer.

FROM HEALTH CANADA'S WEBSITE

http://www.hc-sc.gc.ca

School Sisters of Notre Dame
Celebrating 175 *years*

Spanish Rice with Hamburger

Serves 4

This recipe appeared in the Notre Dame Centenary Cookbook put together by our wonderful "cook" sisters in 1947.

1 pound hamburger
1 cup rice, cooked
1 large tomato, chopped
2 large onions, sliced
1 green pepper, diced

Brown the sliced onion and green pepper in hot fat. Add the well-salted meat and sear well. Add the cooked rice and tomato. Mix all together and bake for one hour in the oven, or, if necessary, longer. Macaroni may be substituted for rice.

183

Submitted by M. Casta, SSND from St. Paul, MN

Spinach Lasagna

Serves 8

1 **pound lasagna noodles,** cooked as directed
1 **pound skim mozzarella,** cut thinly and set aside
3 **eggs,** beaten with fork
1 **medium ricotta cheese,** low fat
1 **pound fresh uncooked spinach,** chopped (frozen is ok)
1 **teaspoon nutmeg**
Salt and pepper, to taste
Handful fresh parsley and basil, chopped
Garlic, chopped
Onions, chopped
184 **Carrot,** cut into slivers (takes acid out of tomatoes)
Mushrooms
8 **cups tomato sauce,** your own or use store bought

Mix together eggs, ricotta cheese, spinach, nutmeg, salt, pepper, parsley and basil.

Sauté garlic, onions, carrot slivers, and mushrooms. Add to the tomato sauce.

Cover bottom of pan with a cup or two of sauce. Layer on top noodles, the egg mixture, and sauce. Repeat until all ingredients are used with sauce on top. Top with slices of mozzarella. Bake covered at 350 for 1 hour and then uncovered at 325 for 30 minutes. Let stand for 15 minutes and serve.

Submitted by Marie Justine Nutz, SSND from Brooklyn NY

Spring Veggie Quiche

Serves 6

1 10 inch piecrust, made from scratch or store bought
1 tablespoon olive oil
1 small onion, finely chopped
½ pound morels or other mushrooms
1 cup asparagus, chopped
or
1 cup fresh spinach leaves, chopped
½ teaspoon salt
Sprinkle black pepper
4 eggs
1½ cups milk
2 tablespoons flour
2 tablespoons fresh dill, chopped
1 cup cheese, grated
Paprika

185

Pre-heat oven to 375 degrees. Heat the olive oil and sauté
onion, mushrooms, asparagus or spinach, salt and pepper. Whisk
together the eggs, milk, flour and dill. On the bottom of the crust,
spread the cheese. Spoon the veggies on top. Add beaten egg
mixture and sprinkle with paprika. Bake for 40-50 minutes or until
solid in the center. Serve hot, warm or at room temperature with
a good crusty bread and a salad of fresh greens or fruit on the
side.

Submitted by Lisa Coons, Director, Center for Earth Spirituality and Rural
Ministry from Mankato, MN

School Sisters of Notre Dame
Celebrating **175** *years*

COOKING *A Celebration of*
EARTH'S GIFTS

St. Louis Bar-B-Que

Serves 8-10

2 pounds stew meat
1 onion, chopped
1 (14-ounce) bottle ketchup
1 teaspoon salt
1 teaspoon sugar
1 green pepper, chopped
1 tablespoon vinegar
1 teaspoon allspice
1 teaspoon dry mustard
½ cup water

186

Put all ingredients in Dutch oven. DO NOT BROWN MEAT. Cover with tight fitting lid. Simmer two hours or until tender. Pull meat into shreds with fork and serve on buns, rice or noodles.

Submitted by Marie Torno, SSND from Chatawa, MS

School Sisters of Notre Dame
Celebrating **175** *years*

Stay-In-Bed Stew

Serves 4-6

1¾ pounds stew meat
¼ cup flour
Salt
Pepper
2 bay leaves
5 stalks celery, cut up
6 carrots, cut up
1 cup green beans, cut up
3 potatoes, cut up
1 can condensed tomato soup, plus a litte water

Spray a casserole dish with non-stick cooking spray. Put in meat, sprinkle with flour, salt, pepper and bay leaves. Add the cut-up celery, carrots, beans, and potatoes. Add tomato soup with a little water. Season to taste. Cover and cook at 275 degrees for 4 hours.

Submitted by Nancy Traeger, SSND from Elm Grove, WI

Stroganoff Crepes

Serves 8-9

1 pound ground beef
Salt and pepper, to taste
1 medium onion, chopped
1 (10.75-ounce) can condensed cream of mushroom soup
2 tablespoons ketchup
4-5 strips bacon, cooked and crumbled
3 green onions, chopped
Mushrooms, chopped (optional)

Cook ground beef with salt, pepper and onions. Drain well. Add mushroom soup, ketchup, bacon, green onion and additional mushrooms, if desired. Mix well and heat thoroughly.

Crepes:
4 eggs
1⅓ cups milk
2 tablespoons oil
1 cup flour
½ teaspoon salt
1 small onion
Cheddar cheese, grated

Put eggs, milk, oil, flour, salt and onion in a blender and mix well. Refrigerate 1 hour. Using a non-stick skillet or a crepe pan sprayed with non-stick cooking spray, fry ½ cup of batter at a time. Turn over to fry other side. Stack with waxed paper between each crepe. Note: Crepe pan needs to be hot when starting.

(continued on next page)

School Sisters of Notre Dame
Celebrating **175** *years*

To assemble: On the lower part of each crepe, place 2-3 heaping tablespoons ground beef mixture. Roll up. Spray 9X13 inch pan with cooking spray. Add crepes and top with grated cheddar cheese. Cover with foil. Bake at 350 for ½ hour. May be frozen and cooked later.

Submitted by Dianne Poitras, Associate from Regina, Saskatchewan, Canada

....

Courtesy
IN THE CONVENT

A small volume "LEST WE FORGET" by School Sisters of Notre Dame (The Newman Press, Westminster, MD 1949) was discovered when closing a convent. The following "morsels" are taken from that book.

". . . , convention, unlike morals, often changes; and in this matter of etiquette at table, it is best and safest to keep up to date. Witness Madame Eglantine of the Canterbury Tales. Of necessity, since all the food was served in one dish in the center of the table, she had to reach for her food. The poet adds, however, that she did so very properly. But today, neither Madam Eglantine nor any well-bred person reaches at all. ***Considerate neighbors anticipate one's need, as indeed they should.***"

"It is true the conventual rules require religious cheerfully to accept the food that is placed before them, ***yet, it does not follow that the culinary department must supply the means of mortification.***"

School Sisters of Notre Dame
Celebrating **175** *years*

Stuffed Salmon

Serves 14 adults

Purchase a salmon large enough for a 6-8-ounce serving per person. Have the butcher butterfly and de-bone the fish. I usually use 2 medium size salmon.

2 medium size salmon

Stuffing:
2 tablespoons olive oil
1 stalk celery, finely chopped, including leaves
1 pound carrots, finely grated
8 ounces fresh mushrooms, sliced
3 cloves garlic, crushed or minced
1 teaspoon oregano
1 teaspoon thyme
1 teaspoon basil
1 teaspoon rosemary
10 slices whole wheat bread, cut into small cubes
2 eggs
1 tablespoon chicken bouillon, dissolved in 1 cup water

In the oil sauté the celery, carrots, mushrooms and garlic. When tender but still crisp add herbs. Finally add bread, eggs and chicken bouillon dissolved in water. Place fish in a glass dish or on a cookie sheet greased with oil. Spoon stuffing mixture onto one side of the fish and gently fold the second side over the mixture.

(continued on next page)

190

School Sisters of Notre Dame
Celebrating **175** *years*

Brush the top of the fish with olive oil. Bake for 1 hour at 325 degrees
or long enough that the fish flakes easily when touched with a fork.
Do not over bake. Serve whole, allowing each person to select their
portion.

Submitted by Kathleen Storms, SSND from Mankato, MN

For those who garden,
the **cycle of planting** and **harvesting**
is an experience *rich*
in the spiritual metaphors.
Gardening enables us
to reflect upon
the **seasons of our own lives**
as we watch
vegetables and fruit mature.

191

The *closer* we are
to the **rhythms** of the **earth,**
the more we are in tune
with our own rhythms,
our personal, inner harmony.
Gardening even a small plot
provides for such reflection upon life's
cycles of birth and death.
In anticipating death through reflection,
we become comfortable with our human
limitedness.

From "The Religious Symbolism of Gardening--a Reflection Upon
the Life-Death Cycle" by Sister Carolyn Sur, SSND, Ph.D.

School Sisters of Notre Dame
Celebrating **175** *years*

Sukiyaki

···

Serves 4

It is said that the name comes from grilling (yaki) meat on a heated hoe (suki). So it is closer to griddle cooking than to simmering, yosenabe-style cooking. Minimal cooking liquid is just enough to cook without burning. This dish is served for the whole family together while it is being cooked at the table. They sit around the skillet and enjoy eating while Sukiyaki is being cooked; this dish unifies the people. This dish is especially tasty in winter, warming up our spirits and bodies. It is also very good with sake.

1⅓ – 2 pounds (600-900 g) beef, sliced
2 ounces beef fat
4 bunches green onions, cut into 2-inch long pieces
1 cake tofu, cubed
1 onion, sliced
1 cup shirataki (konnyaku noodles), parboiled
4 cups Chinese cabbage tops, cut into 2-inch long pieces
1 bunch spinach, cut into 2-inch long pieces
1 cup any type fresh mushrooms
1-2 potatoes, peeled, sliced, and boiled until tender

The best beef for sukiyaki is well marbled prime rib slices. Buy a rib roast and have it boned and sliced ⅛ inch (2-3 mm) thick. Arrange the slices beautifully on a platter with the other ingredients

(continued on next page)

Sauce:
1 cup mirin (sweet sake)
1 cup soy sauce
2 cups sake
2-3 tablespoons sugar (optional)
Combine ingredients

Cooking Sukiyaki: On a hot skillet sear the beef fat, then add some beef slices to the skillet. Pour 1-2 tablespoons sauce over each slice. Add a little water (2 tablespoons). Cover and cook for a few seconds. Uncover and turn meat to cook on the other side. Now the first batch of meat is ready to be eaten.

Add some of the other ingredients to the empty skillet. Top with some beef slices, pour some sauce over the beef, cover and cook for a few minutes. Uncover and turn the meat over. Beef and spinach are the first items to cook, so help yourself when they are just done. Other items will follow, so pick them up and eat as they are done.

193

Push the cooked things to one side of the skillet and add new ingredients to the open area of the skillet. Pour on more sauce. Vegetables exude some juice, but when this liquid has evaporated, add a little water. Also, balance the additions of sauce and water to maintain the correct flavor. Adjust the pace of adding new ingredients to the skillet to match the pace of eating so everyone can enjoy things that have just been freshly cooked.

Submitted by Janet Tanaka, SSND from Kyoto, Japan

Surprise Crock Pot Chicken

Serves 4-6

6-8 chicken legs and/or thighs (breasts work but seem not to be as tasty)
3 tablespoons butter or margarine
1 large onion, chopped
2 cloves garlic, minced
1 teaspoon salt
2 teaspoons paprika
½ teaspoon ground ginger
½ teaspoon chili powder
1 (16-ounce) can tomatoes, crushed or diced
1 can sliced mushrooms (optional)
Couscous, spaghetti or rice

194

Rinse chicken and pat dry. Melt butter in skillet and brown chicken quickly on both sides. Place chicken in crockpot. Stir together remaining ingredients and pour over the chicken. Cover and cook on low 8-10 hours or on high 4-5 hours. Serve on couscous, spaghetti or rice.

Submitted by Carol Marie Hemish, SSND from Buffalo, MN

Sweet-Sour Beef Stew

Serves 6

1½ **pounds beef stew meat**, cut into 1-inch cubes
2 tablespoons cooking oil
2 carrots, shredded
1 cup onion, sliced
1 (8-ounce) can tomato sauce
¼ **cup brown sugar**
¼ **cup vinegar**
1 tablespoon Worcestershire sauce
½ **cup water**
1 teaspoon salt
2 tablespoons cornstarch
1 tablespoon cold water
Noodles, cooked, hot
Poppy seeds (optional)

195

Brown meat in hot oil. Add next 8 ingredients. Cover and cook over low heat until meat is tender, about 1½ hours. Combine cornstarch and 1 tablespoon cold water; add to beef mixture. Cook and stir till thickened and bubbly. Serve over noodles sprinkled with poppy seeds. Garnish with carrot curls and parsley, if desired.

Submitted in 1993 by Regine Collins, SSND from Elm Grove, WI

Swiss Steak Mozzarella

Serves 8

2 pounds round steak, ½ inch thick
3 tablespoons all-purpose flour
¼ cup margarine
1 (16-ounce) can tomatoes
1½ teaspoons salt
¼ teaspoon basil leaves
⅛ teaspoon pepper
½ cup onion, chopped
½ cup green pepper, chopped (red or yellow may also be used)
1½ cups mozzarella cheese, shredded

196

Cut meat into serving-size pieces and then coat with flour. In large covered skillet, melt margarine. Brown meat slowly on all sides. Add tomatoes, salt, basil and pepper. Cover and simmer 1 hour. Add onion and green pepper. Cook 25-30 minutes or until meat is tender. Top meat with cheese. Heat until cheese melts.

Submitted by Joan Frey, SSND from Milwaukee, WI

Share meals with others.
Cook together with friends,
then eat together.

Start a dinner club.

School Sisters of Notre Dame
Celebrating **175** *years*

Taco Meat

Serves 5

*I received this recipe in 1972 from Kay Tushim, a parent of a child at
St. Elizabeth in Dallas. Our favorite way to serve it is with nachos. I also use
it in my squash casserole, stuffed peppers, cheese dip, enchiladas and
anywhere else I think it might enhance a dish. I make 6 pounds at a time
and freeze it in small containers.*

1 pound ground meat, browned
1 large Spanish onion, or another kind of onion
1 clove garlic
1 small tomato (canned, frozen, fresh)
Paprika
½ tablespoon ground cumin
Sugar
Salt and pepper
1 tablespoon picante sauce

197

Brown meat in a skillet. Put onion, garlic and tomato in blender
and blend it together. Add it to the meat. Simmer about one
hour. Season to taste using enough paprika to turn all the meat a
little red. Add cumin and a little sugar. Salt and pepper to taste
and add picante sauce.

Submitted by Sylvia Provost, SSND from North Little Rock, AK

Taco Salad

Serves 8

1½ **pounds ground beef**
1 **medium-size can kidney beans,** drained
1 **head lettuce,** chopped
3 **medium-sized tomatoes,** diced
1 **onion,** chopped
1 **package mild taco seasoning mix**
1 **bag cheddar cheese,** shredded
2 **(8-ounce) bottles Russian dressing**
1 **bag tortilla chips**

198

Brown the ground beef and drain. In a large bowl, place kidney beans, lettuce, tomatoes, onion, taco seasoning and cheddar cheese. Add the browned ground beef. Mix all ingredients together. Pour Russian dressing into mixture. Crumble some chips on top.

May be eaten right away or refrigerate for later. Spoon salad over remaining chips.

Submitted in 1993 by Kenneth Marie Botta, SSND from Baltimore, MD

Tetrazzini

Serves 4-6

8 ounces spaghetti
¼ cup butter or margarine
½ cup flour
2½ cups chicken broth
1 cup light cream or milk
¼ cup sherry
1¼ teaspoons salt
Dash pepper
1 can mushrooms, drained
2 cups chicken or turkey, cooked
½ cup shredded Parmesan cheese   199

Cook spaghetti until tender and drain. In saucepan, melt butter
and blend in flour. Add broth and cream to flour. Mix slowly and
heat until it thickens. Mix together sherry, salt, pepper, mushrooms
and chicken, and add to mixture in saucepan. Pour chicken
sauce over spaghetti and mix well. Put in baking dish. Sprinkle
cheese on top. Bake at 350 degrees for 25 minutes or until hot.
Can be prepared ahead of time and frozen.

Submitted in 1993 by Ruth Speh, SSND from St. Louis, MO (deceased)

Tofu Burgers

Serves 4-6

1 pound soft tofu, drained
2 cups rolled oats, wheat flakes, or barley flakes
1 tablespoon ketchup or barbeque sauce
1 tablespoon Worcestershire sauce
1 small onion, minced
1 teaspoon prepared mustard
1 teaspoon salt
2 dashes pepper
2 tablespoons oil
200 **Garnishes: lettuce, sliced onions, sliced tomatoes, sprouts, pickles**

Mash tofu, mix in oats and blend well. Add all other ingredients, blending well. Wet hands and form thin burgers with the mix, making burgers the size of your bread or roll. Heat oil in skillet. Fry burgers at low heat, about 8 minutes on each side. Serve on buns with garnishes.

Submitted by Suzanne Moynihan, SSND from Mount Calvary, WI

School Sisters of Notre Dame
Celebrating **175** *years*

Tofu Hamburgers

Serves 6

½ **package tofu**
1 **pound ground beef**
1 **tablespoon onion,** chopped
1 **egg yolk**
1 **tablespoon sesame seeds,** toasted
2 **tablespoons Kikkoman soy sauce**
Salt and pepper, to taste

Mix all together and shape into patties, squeezing out any excess
water, and fry. Initially you may need to season the pan with a
little salad oil to keep the tofu burgers from sticking.

201

Submitted by Andrea Ikeda, SSND from Kyoto, Japan

Yahweh, what variety
you have created,

arranging everything so wisely" Ps 104:24

School Sisters of Notre Dame
Celebrating **175** *years*

Tofu Pan Pizza

Serves 4

2 eggs
1 cup soft tofu
1 tablespoon oil
½ teaspoon salt
1½ cups whole wheat flour
2 teaspoons baking powder
1 can pizza sauce
1 cup grated Parmesan cheese
Pizza toppings: green pepper, mushrooms, *whatever you desire*

202

Beat eggs and mash tofu into eggs. Add oil and salt. Mix dry ingredients, then add to tofu mixture and squish with hands. Spread dough on 12-inch oiled pizza pan or baking sheet. Spoon on desired amount of sauce. Add cheese. Add veggies and bake at 400 degrees for 30 minutes.

Note:
If using hard veggies – broccoli, cauliflower, carrots, etc. you may wish to stir fry them first.

Submitted by Suzanne Moynihan, SSND from Mount Calvary, WI

Tuna Chow Mein

Serves 6

1 tablespoon butter or margarine
1 cup celery, diced
¼ cup onion, chopped
2 tablespoons green pepper, chopped
½ (5-ounce) can chow mein noodles, divided
1 can tuna, drained
1 can condensed cream of celery or cream of mushroom soup
¼ cup milk
¼ cup water
⅛ teaspoon pepper
¼ cup salted cashew nuts

203

Heat oven to 350 degrees. Melt butter in large skillet. Add celery, onion and green pepper, and cook until onion is tender. Stir in remaining ingredients except for ¼ cup chow mein noodles. Pour into ungreased 1½ quart casserole dish. Sprinkle remaining chow mein noodles over top. Bake uncovered for 30 minutes.

Submitted by Joan Frey, SSND from Milwaukee, WI

School Sisters of Notre Dame
Celebrating **175** *years*

Upside Down Pizza

Serves 6

1 pound ground beef
¼ teaspoon dried onion
1 can pizza sauce
1 package mozzarella cheese, grated
½ cup sour cream
1 package crescent rolls
⅓ cup Parmesan cheese, grated
1 tablespoon margarine

204

Brown ground beef and drain. Add onion and sauce. Pour into greased 9X13 inch dish. Layer mozzarella cheese, sour cream and crescent rolls. Sprinkle over this Parmesan cheese and margarine. Bake at 375 degrees for 15-20 minutes.

Submitted in 1992 by Mary Margaret Johanning from St. Louis, MO (deceased)

Gallons of water

needed to produce:

One pound of potatoes – 100 gallons
One pound of wheat – 130 gallons
One pound of rice – 340 gallons
One pound of chicken – 460 gallons
One pound of beef – 2,600 gallons

prepared by Religious on Water, ROW, 2005

School Sisters of Notre Dame
Celebrating **175** *years*

Vegetarian Lasagna

Serves 8

16 ounces Ricotta cheese
2 eggs
½ cup Parmesan cheese, grated
1 pound lasagna noodles, cooked as directed
26 ounces spaghetti sauce
3 (10-ounce) packages chopped spinach, cooked
1 pound mozzarella cheese, grated

Mix Ricotta cheese, eggs and Parmesan cheese. Place ⅓ of cooked noodles on bottom of pan. Cover with ⅓ of spaghetti sauce. Put ½ of spinach over sauce. Put ½ of cheese mixture next. Put ⅓ of mozzarella on top of that. Repeat. Place remaining noodles, sauce, and mozzarella on top. Bake uncovered at 350 degrees for 45 minutes.

205

Submitted by Nancy Traeger, SSND from Elm Grove, WI

Virginia Pork Chops

Serves 6

6 pork chops
Salt and pepper
Apple, cored and sliced
Raisins
Brown sugar
Vinegar
Flour

206 Season chops with salt and pepper. Brown in large frying pan, then put them into a 12X18 inch pan. Place slices of cored fresh apple on each chop and fill center of apple with raisins and brown sugar. Make gravy in frying pan with as much vinegar added to drippings as suits your taste, thicken with flour. Pour gravy over chops until they are covered. Cover pan with tin foil and bake at 350 degrees until tender, at least an hour.

Submitted by Esther Mary Atkielski, SSND from Elm Grove, WI

Wild Rice Casserole

Serves 8+

This is a dish that is similar to one I enjoyed with the First Nations people in La Macaza, Quebec.

½ **pound bacon**
½ **pound margarine**
½ **cup onion,** chopped
½ **cup green pepper,** cut up
½ **cup celery,** chopped
1 small can mushrooms
1 small jar pimiento
½ **cup almonds,** sliced
2 cups wild rice, washed and drained, uncooked
½ **teaspoon oregano**
1 teaspoon parsley flakes
4-4½ cups hot chicken broth

Fry bacon and set aside. In margarine, sauté onion, green pepper and celery. When all are cooked, add mushrooms, pimiento, almonds and rice. Continue to sauté until rice begins to crack, then add oregano and parsley flakes. Put all this in large baking dish. Add chicken broth. Bake at 350 degrees for 1-1½ hours or until broth is cooked in.

Submitted by Lynette Friesen, SSND from St. Paul, MN

Bread for the Spirit

by Patricia A. Obremski, SSND

This wood is smooth and warm, and
I am hard-pressed by
hands that are kneading,
needing to reshape, to touch. The silence
of a miracle about to happen hovers
here; my culture shares a memory of
enfolding sourdough and hope, of
unfolding promises fulfilled.
As I expand into the future, I
waft the tang of eras past. Now
pliable and pale, I will
soon exude the scent of crusting,
trusting in the oven's ministry
to finish what is now begun, and then,
fulfillment ... a ritual anointing,
a slathering in yellow, redolent and warm;
a savor shared along with secrets ... as
mother daughter, flowered aprons
floured in remembrance,
join in sisterhood.

208

BAKERY

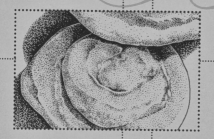

209

from Mother Caroline's pen:

Wisconsin has unbelievably rich farm land. We could call it a blessed bread basket. The people have a surplus of bread and other food items. As they can sell them at a good price, they become prosperous. But right now we are experiencing hard times and a serious shortage of cash. The produce is extremely cheap, and the grain export across the ocean has been completely stopped. The corn merchants and speculators are in serious financial straits, since they receive no capital from Europe. This circumstance puts pressure on commerce and industry. Many people are out of work and out of means for livelihood... the Sisters in our country missions rarely see money, and they are lucky if their needs are taken care of through payment with farm produce. *The Letters of Mother Caroline Friess, School Sisters of Notre Dame, edited by Barbara Brumleve, SSND, p.83*

A Very Good Carmel Roll Sauce

Serves 12-15

⅓ **cup (¾ stick) margarine**
1 cup brown sugar, packed
1 cup vanilla ice cream

In a saucepan, melt the margarine. Add the brown sugar and melt it as well. Add the vanilla ice cream and stir until melted. Do not boil. Spray a 9x13 inch pan with a non-stick cooking spray. Pour the sauce into pan. On top of the sauce, place cinnamon rolls made using your favorite recipe. Bake 350 degrees until golden brown. Turn pan upside down on grate. Cool a few minutes and then remove pan.

212

Submitted by Marguerite Churilla, SSND from St. Cloud, MN

Allewerkenergy Bars: Low-Fat

Makes about 2 dozen

When your work seems tedious and communication breakdowns threaten your equilibrium, why not bake "Allewerkenergy Bars?" Recall Mother Theresa's motto: "All the works of God proceed slowly and in pain; but then their roots are sturdier and their flowering the lovelier." "All the works" is a translation of the German "Alle werke" and seems an appropriate name for energy bars that renew one's spirit after having had a tough day. Allewerkenergy Bars remind us to root our lives in Wisdom greater than ourselves and to celebrate the flowering.

213

¾ **cup brown sugar,** firmly packed
½ **cup granulated sugar**
1 (8-ounce) container of vanilla or plain low-fat yogurt
2 egg whites, lightly beaten
2 tablespoons vegetable oil
2 tablespoons fat-free milk
2 teaspoons vanilla
1½ **cups all-purpose flour**
1 teaspoon baking soda
1 teaspoon ground cinnamon
½ **teaspoon salt** (optional)
3 cups Quaker oats
1 cup dried fruit, raisins or cranberries, chopped
⅓ **cup applesauce**

Heat oven to 350 degrees. In large bowl combine sugars, yogurt, egg whites, oil, milk and vanilla. In a separate bowl, combine flour, baking soda, cinnamon, salt and oats. Add to the creamed mixture mixing well. *(continued on next page)*

Stir in the fruit. Spread batter into an ungreased 13x9 inch baking pan. Bake 30 minutes or until it's a light golden brown. Cool completely on a wire rack. Cut into bars and store in a tightly covered tin.

As a little extra treat, take **1 cup of powdered sugar and add 2-3 teaspoons of real lemon juice.** Stir to the consistency that is good for spreading on the hot bars right after they come out of the oven. This gives a little tang to the bars.

Submitted by Judy Best, SSND from Washington, MO

Creation

"GOD saw that it **was GOOD**." Genesis 1:10

214

Environmental issues are not separate from overall human concerns. The health of the air, soil, water, and wildlife are directly related to our own health, and to that of our children and grandchildren.

Modern agribusiness is focused on producing large quantities at low financial cost.

"Sustainable agriculture" is focused on creating a system that can go on indefinitely. It must be economically viable, but it also must care for the land and provide a good quality of life for all.

Simply in Season Study Guide
www.worldcommunitycookbook.org/season/studyguide.html

School Sisters of Notre Dame
Celebrating **175** *years*

Angel Macaroons

Makes 2 dozen

1 (16-ounce) package one-step white angel food cake mix
½ cup water or sugar-free strawberry or orange-flavored soda
1½ teaspoons almond extract
1 (7-ounce) package shredded coconut

Heat oven to 350 degrees. Cover a cookie sheet with brown paper. Beat cake mix, water and almond extract in large bowl on low speed, scraping bowl constantly for 30 seconds. Then beat on medium speed, scraping bowl occasionally for 1 minute. Fold in coconut. Drop batter by measuring teaspoons about 2 inches apart onto covered cookie sheet. Bake until set, about 10-12 minutes. Slide paper, with cookies, onto wire rack; cool cookies completely before removing from paper.

215

Note: I often find the cookies almost impossible to remove if I let them set on the paper. I usually remove them from the paper about 30 seconds after I remove them from the oven.

Submitted in 1993 by Marie Richard Eckerle, SSND from Chatawa, MS

Baked Boston Brown Bread

Makes 3 small loaves

2 tablespoons butter, softened
½ cup brown sugar
2 eggs
2½ teaspoons baking soda
1½ cups sour milk/buttermilk
1 teaspoon salt
½ cup dark molasses
1 cup white flour
3 cups bran
⅓ cup nuts, cut up
1 cup raisins

216

Cream butter and sugar well; add eggs and beat. Combine baking soda and sour milk; add to the first mixture. Add remaining ingredients. Put into three small greased baking powder cans or one large loaf pan. Be sure to leave at least one inch between mixture and top of pan. Bake at 325 degrees for one hour or longer if using loaf pan. Cool in pan about 10 minutes before removing.

Submitted by Agnes Marie Schulte, SSND from Chatawa, MS (deceased)

Banana Bread

Makes 2 loaves

3½ **cups flour**
2½ **teaspoons baking powder**
½ **teaspoon salt**
1 **tablespoon baking soda**
1⅔ **cups sugar**
⅔ **cup margarine**
4 **eggs**
⅔ **cup milk**
2 **cups bananas**, mashed
½ **cup pecans**, chopped

217

In a mixing bowl, sift flour, baking powder, salt and baking soda. Set aside. Cream sugar and margarine, add eggs and milk beating until smooth and fluffy. Add flour mixture and mashed bananas alternately to creamed mixture beating smooth after each addition. Gently fold in pecans.

Turn batter into two greased and floured loaf pans. Bake in 350 degree oven 60 to 65 minutes. If using a convection oven, set the oven at 300 and bake for 50+ minutes Cool in pan 10 minutes. Remove from pan and cool thoroughly.

Submitted by Odile Poliquin, SSND from St. Louis, MO

Beer Bread

Makes 1 loaf

This is very easy and does not require kneading or rising time before baking.

2 tablespoons sugar
1 (12-ounce) can beer
3 cups self-rising flour

Blend sugar into beer. Stir in flour one cup at a time. Grease loaf pan. Pour in batter. Bake at 350 degrees for 1 hour. Cool in pan for 10 minutes. Remove from pan and cool thoroughly.

218

Submitted by Joan Frey, SSND from St. Louis, MO

customs & traditions

School Sisters of Notre Dame observed customs and traditions which served to remind us of God's goodness and respect for creation.

"When I entered the School Sisters of Notre Dame in Wilton, Connecticut in 1963, we were taught to observe this custom: when you take a piece of bread or roll from the plate, kiss the bread as a sign of gratitude to God for all food. This custom reminded me of something I had learned at home. We were taught as children always to place the bread properly on the table, never on its side or upside down. Again, this was a sign of respect for the bread, for food, and gratitude that we had food to eat."

Grace L. D'Amico, SSND

School Sisters of Notre Dame
Celebrating **175** *years*

Boston Brown Bread

Makes 3 loaves

1 quart (4.5 cups) flour
1 quart (4.5 cups) All Bran
1½ cups sugar
2 cups Grandma's molasses
1 teaspoon salt
1 teaspoon baking powder
1 teaspoon baking soda
1 quart (4 cups) buttermilk or sour milk
nuts and/or raisins (optional)

Mix all ingredients and pour into well-greased pans leaving room
for dough to rise. Bake in moderate 350 degree oven for 1½ hours.
Nuts and raisins may be added as desired.

Submitted in 1993 by Leocadia Meyer, SSND from St. Louis, MO (deceased)

Bran Molasses Muffins

Makes 12 muffins

This recipe appeared in the Notre Dame Centenary Cookbook put together by our wonderful "cook" Sisters in 1947.

2 cups whole bran
½ cup light molasses
1½ cups milk
1 egg
1 cup flour
½ teaspoon salt
1 teaspoon soda

220

Add whole bran to molasses and milk and allow to soak for 15 minutes. Beat egg and add to first mixture. Sift flour, salt, and soda together and combine with whole bran mixture. Fill greased muffin pans ½ full and bake about 20 minutes in a moderately hot oven of 400 degrees.

Submitted by M. George Gentile, SSND from Chicago, IL (deceased)

Brownies

Serves 9

2 tablespoons margarine
1 square unsweetened baking chocolate
½ cup sugar
1 egg
½ teaspooon vanilla
⅓ cup flour, unsifted
2 tablespoons walnuts, chopped

Combine margarine and chocolate square in 2-cup glass measure. Microwave on high about 1½ minutes or until chocolate is melted, stirring once. Add sugar, egg and vanilla. Stir in flour and nuts. Mix well. Spread batter evenly in an ungreased 5-inch square baking dish that is microwave-safe. Cover with plastic wrap. Microwave on high about 2½ minutes or until no longer doughy. Rotate dish once. Cool. Cut into squares.

221

Submitted by Joan Bartosh, SSND from Rochester, MN

Chocolate Bread

Makes 2 loaves

2 packages yeast
¼ cup warm water
1 teaspoon sugar
2 cups milk
4 tablespoons shortening, melted
½ cup sugar
1½ teaspoons salt
2 eggs, well beaten
7 tablespoons cocoa
7½ cups flour

Dissolve yeast in ¼ cup water and 1 teaspoon sugar. Warm milk and add melted shortening. Put 4 cups flour in large bowl. Add milk mixture, dissolved yeast, sugar, salt, eggs and cocoa. Mix together. Stir in 2 cups more flour. Knead in the remaining flour or enough to make a soft dough. Let rise. Knead down and let rise again. Make into 2 loaves. Let rise. Bake for 1 hour at 350 degrees.

Submitted by Joan Bartosh, SSND from Rochester, MN

Chocolate Mint Cookies

Makes 100 cookies

1½ cups margarine
3 cups brown sugar
4 tablespoons water
4 cups semi-sweet chocolate chips
2 eggs
5 cups flour
2½ teaspoons baking soda
1 teaspoon salt
2 boxes Andes candy mints

223

Cook margarine, brown sugar, and water until melted. Add chocolate chips and stir until melted. Put mixture into a mixing bowl. Let stand 10–15 minutes to cool. Add eggs, one at a time, mixing at high speed. Reduce speed to low. Add dry ingredients and beat until blended. Chill dough 1½ hours. Form dough into balls and place on an ungreased cookie sheet. Bake at 350 degrees for 8–10 minutes. Remove from oven; while still hot place a half of an Andes Candy on top of each cookie. Once the mint is soft, swirl around top of cookie.

Submitted by Pat Murphy, SSND from Elm Grove, WI

Chocolate Pecan Cookies

Makes 8 dozen cookies

From my mother, Laura Smith Poliquin.

1 cup butter or margarine, softened
2 cups sugar
2 eggs, well beaten
4 cups flour
4 teaspoons baking powder
8 tablespoons cocoa
4 cups pecans, chopped
2 cups milk

224

Cream butter and sugar; add eggs. Sift, measure and sift flour again with other dry ingredients and chopped nuts. Combine alternately dry ingredients and milk with the first mixture. Drop by spoonfuls onto cookie sheet. You can substitute chocolate chips for pecans. Bake 10-12 minutes in 350 degree oven.

Submitted by Odile Poliquin, SSND from St. Louis, MO

Chocolate Walnut Loaf

Makes 2 loaves

1 teaspoon soda
1 cup buttermilk
5 eggs
2 cups sugar
¼ teaspoon salt
2 squares unsweetened chocolate, melted
1 teaspoon anise or vanilla flavor
2¼ cups flour
1 cup walnuts, chopped

Combine soda with buttermilk. Then mix all ingredients in order given. Pour into two 9x5x3 inch loaf pans greased and lightly floured. Bake at 325 degrees for one hour or until done.

225

Submitted by Kathleen Storms, SSND from Mankato, MN

Chocolate Zucchini Muffins

Makes 24 muffins

2½ cups flour
¼ cup cocoa
1 teaspoon salt
½ teaspoon baking powder
1 teaspoon baking soda
¼ cup flaxseed, ground
½ cup margarine
¼ cup canola oil
1½ cups granulated sugar
2 eggs
½ cup sour milk or buttermilk
2 cups zucchini, unpeeled, grated

226

Preheat oven to 350 degrees. In a bowl, combine flour, cocoa, salt, baking powder, baking soda and ground flaxseed. In a separate bowl, cream margarine, canola oil and sugar. Add eggs and sour milk. Add flour mixture, stirring until just mixed. Add zucchini and mix. Fill greased and floured muffin cups half to two-thirds full. Bake 18-20 minutes or until wooden toothpick inserted comes out clean. Remove and cool on rack.

Submitted by Joan Bartosh, SSND from Rochester, MN

Chow Mein Cookies

Makes 2-3 dozen

1 cup chocolate chips
1 cup butterscotch chips
3 cups chow mein noodles
½ cup peanuts or cashews

Melt chips slowly until they form a pudding. Then immediately add the chow mein noodles and salted peanuts or cashews. Spoon onto waxed paper and cool. Store in cookie tins in the refrigerator.

Submitted by Rita Mary Schweihs, SSND from Homer Glen, IL

227

Let us live in a way
**which will not
deprive other beings**
OF AIR, WATER, FOOD, SHELTER,
or the chance
TO LIVE.

Thich Nhat Hahn

School Sisters of Notre Dame
Celebrating **175** *years*

Christmas Bread

Makes 2 loaves

½ **cup margarine**
1½ **cups sugar**
8 **ounces cream cheese**
1 **teaspoon vanilla**
4 **eggs**
2½ **cups flour**
2 **teaspoons baking powder**
1 **cup nuts**
1 **cup maraschino cherries,** cut and drained

228

Cream margarine, sugar, cream cheese, and vanilla. Add eggs, flour, and baking powder. Add nuts and cherries. Grease and flour pans. Bake at 350 degrees for 1 hour.

Submitted by Joan Frey, SSND from St. Louis, MO

MANY THINGS
grow in the garden
that were
NEVER
sown there.
Anonymous

School Sisters of Notre Dame
Celebrating **175** *years*

Christmas Stollen

Makes 1 stollen for 15 servings

Put **1 package dry yeast** into **½ cup warm water.**
   Add **¼ teaspoon sugar.**
   Let rise 5 minutes in a warm place.

To **1 cup** scalded **milk** add:
   ½ cup sugar
   ½ cup melted **butter or margarine**
   2 eggs, beaten

To **4½ cups flour** add:
   ½ teaspoon salt
   ½ cup raisins
   ⅔ cup mixed candied fruit
   ¼ cup nuts, chopped

229

Add dry ingredients to liquids, a small amount at a time, stirring well. Let rise 1 hour and punch down. Knead. Let rise another ½ hour.

Roll out in an oval shape ¾ inch thick. Crease oval dough lengthwise off center, butter larger side. Fold over smaller part.

Put on a greased pan and let rise till double in size. Butter the top. When risen, bake at 350 degrees for 30-35 minutes or until brown.

Frost, and top with **chopped nuts and maraschino cherries.**

Submitted in 1993 by M. Evidia, SSND from Chicago, IL (deceased)

School Sisters of Notre Dame
Celebrating **175** *years*

Chruszczki

Makes 2-3 dozen

12 egg yolks
3 whole eggs
2 tablespoons vinegar
3 tablespoons sugar
½ teaspoon salt
3 cups flour
Powdered sugar
Oil for frying

230

Beat egg yolks, whole eggs, vinegar, sugar and salt together.
Add flour. Add more flour if needed to make a stiff dough.
Mix well and roll out very thin. Cut in strips about 4 inches x 1 inch.
Twist. Fry in deep fat. Drain on brown paper bag. Sprinkle with
powdered sugar.

Submitted by Dolorita Sierszynski, SSND from Mount Calvary, WI

While Jesus was at table with them,
He took bread and said the blessing
AND BROKE IT,
and handed it to them.
And their eyes were opened
and they recognized Him.
Luke 29:29-31

School Sisters of Notre Dame
Celebrating **175** *years*

Cottage Cheese Crescents

Makes 4 dozen

1 pound (2 cups) small curd cottage cheese (4% milk fat)
1 cup (2 sticks) margarine
2 cups flour
Powdered sugar
Almond flavoring

Have cottage cheese and margarine at room temperature. Mix well. Add flour and mix until smooth.

Refrigerate overnight. Divide dough into four portions. Form each portion into a ball. On a floured surface, roll each ball into a 12 inch circle. Cut each circle into 12 wedges. Beginning at outer edge, roll each wedge into a crescent. Place on ungreased baking sheet with tip underneath. Repeat with three remaining balls. Bake at 350 degrees for 30-35 minutes until crescents are slightly brown and speckled.   Remove from pan. When cool, frost with powdered sugar icing flavored with almond extract.

231

Submitted by Regine Collins, SSND from Elm Grove, WI

School Sisters of Notre Dame
Celebrating **175** *years*

Crullers

Serves 4

This is a recipe from my mom.

2 eggs
1 cup sugar
4 cups flour
3 teaspoons baking powder
1 teaspoon salt
¼ teaspoon nutmeg
1 cup milk
Oil for frying

232

In a large bowl beat eggs until creamy; add sugar gradually.
Sift flour, baking powder, salt and nutmeg in a separate bowl.
Add alternately to egg mixture, the dry ingredients and milk.
Add more flour until you can roll out the dough. Cut dough into
4-inch long strips and braid. Fry in deep fat.

Best served with hot tomato soup:

Cook cubed beef with onion in water. Add 2 (8-ounce) cans
tomato sauce and 2 cans water. Then add 1 cup of rice. Cook
until rice is tender. Then add 1 or 2 cups of noodles and cook
again until tender. (Canned tomatoes, fresh tomatoes and more
water can be added if desired.)

Submitted by Charlene Zeisset, SSND from St. Louis, MO

Farewell Coffee Cake

Serves 12-16

I call this a farewell coffee cake since I made it as a treat for the provincial office staff in Dallas before I left in June 2006.

⅔ **cup margarine**
1 **cup granulated sugar**
½ **cup brown sugar**, packed
2 **eggs**
2 **cups flour**
1 **teaspoon baking powder**
1 **teaspoon baking soda**
1 **teaspoon ground cinnamon**
½ **teaspoon salt**
1 **cup buttermilk** (1 cup milk plus 1 tablespoon white vinegar, mixed well, may be used in place of buttermilk)

233

Cream margarine and sugars together until smooth.
Add eggs, one at a time, mixing after each addition.
Mix the dry ingredients. Add half the dry mixture and then half the buttermilk to the egg mixture and mix. Add remaining dry ingredients and buttermilk and mix well. Spread in 9x13 inch greased pan. Sprinkle topping over the batter. Cover lightly and refrigerate overnight or for a least 8 hours. Bake uncovered in 350 degree oven for 30-35 minutes. Cut into squares and serve warm or at room temperature. Can be served for breakfast, lunch or dinner. Store leftovers in a covered container.

(continued on next page)

Topping:

½ **cup brown sugar,** packed
¾ **cup pecans or walnuts,** chopped
½ **teaspoon ground cinnamon**
¼ **teaspoon ground nutmeg**

Combine all ingredients in a bowl; mix well. Sprinkle over the batter.

Submitted by Jacqueline Buckley, SSND from Milwaukee, WI

A Mug of Coffee

Patricia A. Obremski, SSND

Warm
and welcoming…
I hold you reverently
between my eager palms…
mist curling outward in
the chill of dawn.
Rich
and brown and holy…
your aroma tempts me
to sip, to
risk my lips,
my tongue in eagerness to
gratify my longing.
Deep
and still and waiting…
spirit, cupped and working
in the mystery of beans,
sacrificed
and steeped,
you energize to transformation.

With abandon,
I savor every sip!

Flaxseed Bread

Makes 1 loaf for 10-12 servings

1 tablespoon active dry yeast
1¾ cups warm water
3 tablespoons honey (or ⅛ cup sugar)
1 tablespoon oil (safflower or olive)
½ teaspoon salt
1 cup flaxseed meal (or ⅔ cup whole seeds, ground)
3 cups whole wheat flour, freshly ground
1-2 tablespoons gluten (for higher rising loaf) (optional)

In a large bowl, dissolve yeast in the warm water. Set aside until bubbly, about 5 minutes. Mix in the honey, oil, salt, flaxseed meal, and half of the flour. Mix well. Stir in the rest of the flour and gluten, adding about ½ cup at a time until the dough is soft and kneadable. Turn the dough onto a lightly floured surface. Knead for about 10 minutes until smooth and elastic. Grease a 9x5 inch bread pan. Shape the dough into a loaf and place in the pan. Cover and let rise in a warm place for about an hour until doubled in size. Bake at 350 degrees for 40-45 minutes or until the loaf is brown on top and sounds hollow when tapped. Cool for 10 minutes and then remove from pan.

235

Submitted by Rita Marie Schneider, SSND from Mankato, MN

Flaxseed

is a nutty-flavored grain
that is rich in heart-healthy
omega-3 fats. Europeans have baked with
this crunchy treasure for years.

School Sisters *of* Notre Dame
Celebrating **175** *years*

Francette's Banana Chocolate Chip Bread

Makes 4 bread-pan loaves or 9 mini-pan loaves

Besides being very delicious, this recipe stays moist for a very long time.

½ **cup butter**
½ **cup shortening**
2 **cups sugar**
4 **eggs**
2 **cups all-purpose flour**
2 **cups whole wheat flour**
2 **teaspoons baking soda**
½ **teaspoon baking powder**
1 **teaspoon cinnamon**
4 **cups bananas,** well ripened, mashed
1 **cup chocolate chips**
1 **cup nuts** (optional)

Cream butter, shortening and sugar. Add eggs and beat well.
Mix all dry ingredients together. Alternate adding dry ingredients
and bananas to creamed mixture. Add chocolate chips and
nuts (if used). Pour into 9 oiled mini tins or 4 oiled bread pans.
Bake at 350 degrees for 45 minutes or until done.

Submitted by Francette Malecha, SSND from Cambridge, MN

236

German-Irish Soda Bread

Makes 5 small loaves serving 8-10

This is a bit modified from a recipe given to me by a French sister from the Congregation of Notre Dame.

1 cup raisins
1 cup boiling water
4 cups flour
½ teaspoon cream of tartar
1 teaspoon salt
1 tablespoon baking powder
1 teaspoon baking soda
2 tablespoons caraway seed
⅔ cup sugar
2 tablespoons vegetable oil
2 beaten eggs
2 cups buttermilk

237

Cover raisins in 1 cup boiling water for 10 minutes. Mix flour, cream of tartar, salt, baking powder and baking soda. Add raisins (drained), caraway seeds and sugar. Combine oil, beaten eggs, buttermilk. Mix all together and turn into small greased loaf pans. Bake 1 hour at 350 degrees.

Submitted by Marie Justine Nutz, SSND from Brooklyn, NY

A woman is like a tea bag. The longer she is in hot water, the stronger she gets!
Eleanor Roosevelt, First Lady 1933-1945

School Sisters of Notre Dame
Celebrating **175** *years*

Gift of the Magi Bread

Makes 2 loaves

1 cup sugar
½ cup butter
2 eggs
1 teaspoon vanilla
2 cups flour
1 teaspoon baking soda
¼ teaspoon salt
1 cup **bananas**, mashed
½ cup **dates**, chopped
1 can mandarin oranges
1 cup chocolate chips
1 cup coconut
⅔ cup **nuts**, chopped
½ cup **maraschino cherries**, chopped

238

Preheat oven to 350 degrees. Cream together sugar, butter, eggs and vanilla. Add flour, soda and salt to mixture alternately with mashed bananas. Stir in remaining ingredients. Pour into 2 greased loaf pans (7½ x 3¾ inches). Bake about 1 hour.

Submitted by Odile Poliquin, SSND from St. Louis, MO

Ginger Bread Muffins

Makes 12 muffins

¼ cup butter
1 egg
⅔ cup sour milk
1 teaspoon baking soda
1 teaspoon cinnamon
½ cup sugar
½ cup molasses
1½ cups flour
1 teaspoon ginger

Mix all ingredients. Place in greased muffin tins. Bake at **239**
350 degrees for 20 minutes.

Submitted in 1993 by Marie Rose Van Deurzen, SSND from Manawa, WI

If **you have two coins** *and* **use one to buy** *a loaf of* **bread** *to feed the POOR;* **use the other** *to buy a* **hyacinth** *to feed* YOUR SOUL. *Hindu Proverb*

School Sisters of Notre Dame
Celebrating **175** *years*

Ginger Snaps

Makes 8 dozen cookies

1½ **cups shortening** (butter or margarine)
2 **cups sugar**
2 **eggs**
½ **cup molasses**
4 **cups flour**
2 **teaspoons baking soda**
2 **teaspoons cinnamon**
2 **teaspoons cloves**
2 **teaspoons ginger**
Salt
Extra sugar for dipping

240

Cream shortening and sugar. Beat in eggs. Add molasses and sifted dry ingredients. Shape into balls and dip one side in sugar. Place dipped or sugared dough side up on cookie sheet. Will flatten in oven. Bake at 375 degrees for 15-18 minutes.

Submitted by Dolorita Sierszynski, SSND from Mount Calvary, WI

Healthy Oatmeal Cookies

Makes 15 large cookies

2 cups rolled oats
2 cups whole wheat flour
1 ripe banana, mashed
½ cup raisins, soaked overnight then drained
1 cup honey
1½ cups cold water or apple cider
2 teaspoons lemon juice
2 tablespoons molasses

Mix together dry ingredients. Mix together moist ingredients.
Add moist to dry. Stir together. Drop by spoonfuls on oiled
cookie sheets and bake at 350 degrees until browned.

241

Submitted by Suzanne Moynihan, SSND from Mount Calvary, WI

"**Lord**, *to those who hunger,*
give **bread**
and to those who have bread,
give **a hunger** for **justice.**"

Latin American Prayer

School Sisters of Notre Dame
Celebrating **175** *years*

Healthy Peanut Butter Cookies

Makes 3 dozen

½ **cup margarine**
½ **cup peanut butter**
½ **cup granulated sugar**
½ **cup brown sugar,** packed
1 egg
1¼ **cup all purpose flour**
½ **teaspoon baking powder**
¼ **teaspoon salt**
¾ **teaspoon baking soda**

242

Mix thoroughly: margarine, peanut butter, sugars and egg. *or not*
Measure flour by dipping method or by sifting. Blend all dry
ingredients; stir into peanut butter mixture. Chill dough. Heat
oven to 375 degrees. Roll dough into ¼ inch balls. Place 3 inches
apart on lightly greased baking sheet. With fork dipped in flour,
flatten crisscross style. Bake 10-12 minutes.

Submitted by Mary Serafine Della Croce, SSND from Trumbull, CT

Makes about 3½ doz. lrg. cookies.

Indian Bread

Serves 12

1½ cups water
½ cup cornmeal
2 teaspoons salt
6 tablespoons margarine
½ cup molasses
2½ packages yeast
1 teaspoon sugar
1 cup warm water
6 cups flour

In a saucepan, mix the 1½ cups water, cornmeal, salt, margarine
and molasses. Bring to a boil and continue cooking and stirring
until the mixture thickens. Cool. In a separate bowl dissolve yeast
and sugar in the warm water. Add to thickened mixture. Add
flour, 2 cups at a time, until you have a soft dough. Knead
10 minutes. Let rise until double. Knead down. Let rise again.
Form into 2 round loaves. Roll each loaf in corn meal. Place
into two greased, round casserole dishes. Let rise. Bake at
350 degrees for 45 minutes.

243

Submitted by Joan Bartosh, SSND from Rochestser, MN

Irish Soda Bread

Makes 5 loaves

This is one of the favorites at the Motherhouse in St. Louis.

5 pounds flour
5 tablespoons baking powder
5 teaspoons baking soda
3 cups sugar
Salt
1½ quarts sour cream
10 eggs
2 cups buttermilk
4 cups raisins

Combine the dry ingredients: flour, baking powder, baking soda, sugar and salt. Then mix in the rest of the ingredients: sour cream, eggs, buttermilk, and finally the raisins. Spray the bread pans with cooking spray. Divide the dough into 5 pans. After the dough is in the pan, cut a cross with a sharp knife in the top of each loaf. Bake at 350 degrees for 45 minutes to an hour.

Note: One pound of flour = 4 cups
One quart = 4 cups

Submitted by Odile Poliquin, SSND from St. Louis, MO

Kitchen Sink Cookies

Makes 7 dozen cookies

You can add just about anything to this recipe as a substitute for the Rice Krispies and coconut.

1 cup white sugar
1 cup brown sugar
1 cup butter, softened
1 cup oil
1 egg
3½ cups flour
1½ teaspoons baking soda
1 teaspoon cream of tartar
½ teaspoon salt
1 cup oatmeal
1 cup semisweet chocolate chips
1 cup Rice Krispies
½ to 1 cup shredded coconut

245

Cream together white sugar, brown sugar, butter and oil, add egg. In a separate bowl, combine flour, baking soda, cream of tartar and salt. Mix with creamed ingredients. Add oatmeal, chocolate chips, Rice Krispies and coconut. Drop by rounded teaspoons on ungreased cookie sheet. Bake at 350 degrees for 10-12 minutes.

Submitted by Odile Poliquin, SSND from St. Louis, MO

Lemon Bread

....

Makes 3-4 small loaves

1 package lemon 2-layer cake mix
1 package instant vanilla pudding
or
1 package yellow 2-layer cake mix
1 package instant lemon pudding
1 cup water
½ cup oil
4 eggs

246 Mix together cake mix, pudding mix, water, oil and eggs until
moist, about 4 minutes. Grease or spray with cooking spray
3 or 4 small loaf pans. Divide batter equally among them so
that pans are ¾ full. Bake at 350 degrees for about 40 minutes.

Glaze:
1 cup powdered sugar
1 tablespoon margarine, melted
2 tablespoons lemon juice

Melt margarine in saucepan. Remove from heat. Blend in
the powdered sugar. Stir in lemon juice, a teaspoon at a time
until glaze is of proper consistency to drizzle. Use more juice as
needed to form a thin glaze.

Poke holes over top of the hot loaves with a fork and drizzle glaze
over the top.   Add poppy seeds to make Lemon Poppy Seed
Bread

Submitted by Marguerite Churilla, SSND from St. Cloud, MN

Maul Dorshen
....

Makes 12

This was one of my dad's favorite recipes that his mother made. Mom had to learn to make it as good as grandma's. Now I am trying to make it as good as mom's.

2 cups flour
½ cup shortening
1 egg
1 teaspoon salt
1 cup sugar
4 tablespoons cold water
¾ cup raisins
½ teaspoon cinnamon
¼ cup sugar
2 tablespoons butter or margarine
2 cups milk
¼ cup sugar
½ teaspoon cinnamon

247

Mix together the flour, shortening, egg, salt, 1 cup sugar and water as for a pie crust. Divide dough in thirds and roll each one into a rectangle (4x12 inch). Mix together the raisins, cinnamon, ¼ cup sugar and butter, and sprinkle on each section.

(continued on next page)

Fold two sides toward center and pinch together. Lay all three folded sections side by side in a 9x13 inch pan. Pour milk over rolls and sprinkle with sugar and cinnamon. Bake at 325 degrees for 40-45 minutes.

Submitted by Kathleen Storms, SSND from Mankato, MN

Rebirth *of the* Red Bar.

by Lois Wickenhauser, SSND

Written about the red barn at Good Counsel, Mankato, MN when it was in danger of being demolished. It was preserved, repaired and continues to be a landmark on the Hill!

Lonely on the landscape
abandoned like a forgotten toy
when efficiency was crowned godde

Too proud to surrender
though rumors and threats
strained to demolish.

You waited
pregnant with hope
sustained with memories.

Hands gentle with strength
reverent with power
over wood and stone
had birthed you
cathedral-like.

Trinitarian in structure
destined to cradle
nurturing relationships
your wounded spirit
embraced the past
caressing sacred memories.

Waiting.........Hoping.......

Resilient and reconciled
you invite us again
to relationship
to rituals
to promise.

Moist Chewy Brownies

Serves 12

4 tablespoons cocoa
1 tablespoon canola oil
½ cup butter, room temperature
1 cup sugar
2 eggs
1 teaspoon vanilla
½ cup flour
½ teaspoon salt
⅓ cup chocolate chips
⅓ cup walnuts or pecans, chopped

249

Combine cocoa and oil. Add the butter, sugar, eggs and vanilla.
Beat well. Stir in the flour and salt. Add chocolate chips and nuts.
Bake in an 8-inch square pan at 350 degrees for 25 minutes or
until a toothpick comes out clean from the center of the pan.
I like to frost this with fudge frosting and sprinkle nut pieces on top.

Submitted by Joan Bartosh, SSND from Rochester, MN

Morning Glory Muffins

Makes 30 muffins

From a friend, Betty Brandvold.

4 cups flour
1 cup sugar
1 cup brown sugar
4 teaspoons baking soda
4 teaspoons cinnamon
Salt
4 cups carrots, grated
1 cup raisins
1 cup coconut
2 apples, grated
6 eggs, beaten
2 cups oil
4 teaspoons vanilla
1 cup nuts, chopped

250

In a bowl, mix flour, sugars, baking soda, cinnamon and salt. Stir in grated carrots, raisins, coconut and grated apples. In another bowl, mix the eggs, oil and vanilla. Stir this into the flour mixture until the batter is just combined. Add the nuts. Spoon into greased muffin tins and bake at 350 degrees for 25 minutes.

Submitted by Odile Poliquin, SSND from St. Louis, MO

Oatmeal Chocolate Chip Cookies

Makes about 4½ dozen

Fibre and flavour in one delectable package!

⅔ **cup margarine**
½ **cup granulated sugar**
½ **cup brown sugar**, lightly packed
2 eggs
1½ **cups whole wheat flour**
1 teaspoon baking soda
½ **teaspoon salt**
3 cups rolled oats
½ **cup walnuts**, chopped
½ **cup chocolate chips**

251

Cream together margarine and sugars until light and creamy.
Beat in the eggs one at a time. In a bowl, mix together flour,
baking soda and salt, then stir this into the creamed mixture. Add
the rolled oats, walnuts, and chocolate chips. Mix well. Drop
by teaspoonfuls onto a lightly oiled or paper-lined cookie sheet.
Bake at 350 degrees for 10-12 minutes or until golden brown.

Submitted by Andre Hogan, SSND from Waterdown, Ontario, Canada

School Sisters of Notre Dame
Celebrating **175** *years*

Oatmeal Cookies

Makes 2 dozen large cookies

I received this recipe while visiting Santuaro Sisterfarm in Texas. Sanctuario Sisterfarm is a sanctuary for cultivating diversity and living in right relationship with the whole earth community. (www.sisterfarm.org)

1 cup (2 sticks) unsalted butter, softened
1½ cups dark brown sugar, packed
2 tablespoons honey
2 eggs
1½ cups unbleached all-purpose flour
1 tablespoon ground cinnamon
1 teaspoon salt
4 cups old fashioned oats
¾ cup dates, chopped
¾ cup raisins
1½ cups pecans, chopped
Other dried fruit and nuts to taste, chopped

252

Preheat oven to 375 degrees and grease cookie sheets. Cream together butter, brown sugar and honey. Beat in eggs one at a time. Sift together the flour, cinnamon and salt. Stir this into butter mixture with wooden spoon. Add oats, dried fruit and nuts. Stir until well mixed. Shape dough into 2 inch balls, place on sheets, then flatten to make large cookies. Bake until lightly browned, about 15 minutes. Immediately remove cookies onto wire racks to cool.

Submitted by Patricia Murphy, SSND from Elm Grove, WI

Oh Henry Bars

Makes 32 bars

⅔ cup margarine
4 cups quick cooking oatmeal
1 cup brown sugar
2 teaspoons vanilla
½ cup dark or light corn syrup

In a bowl mix together the ingredients. Pour into a greased
9X13 inch pan and bake for 12 minutes at 350 degrees. Mixture
will be bubbly when removed from oven. Allow to cool before
spreading on the topping. You may also sprinkle peanuts on top.
Refrigerate. Cut into bars when cool.

253

Topping:
1 cup chocolate chips
⅔ cup peanut butter

Melt the chips and then mix in the peanut butter.

Submitted by Mary Kerber, SSND in Nairobi, Kenya

Pancakes

Serves 4

2 eggs, separated
1 teaspoon sugar
½ teaspoon salt
1 cup milk
1 cup flour
½ teaspoon baking soda

Mix egg yolks, sugar, salt, milk, flour, soda.
Beat egg whites with beater until soft peak. Fold in.

254

Heat griddle or skillet over medium heat, 375 degrees. Grease skillet with butter or oil as necessary. For each pancake, pour less than ¼ cup batter onto hot griddle or skillet. Cook pancake until bubbly on top, puffed and dry around the edges. Turn and cook other side until golden brown.

Submitted by Marie Rose VanDeurzen, SSND from Manawa, WI

Come, **Blessed of God,**
for I was hungry and you gave me food.
I was thirsty and you gave me drink.

Matthew 25:34-35

School Sisters of Notre Dame
Celebrating **175** *years*

Parker House Rolls

Makes 2 dozen

This recipe appeared in a cookbook put together by the 1901 class of the Academy of Our Lady (A.O.L.) in 1925 to raise money for the chapel.

4 cups flour
1 teaspoon salt
6 teaspoons baking powder
4 tablespoons shortening, melted
1½ cups milk
Butter, melted

255

Sift flour, salt and baking powder together. Add melted shortening to milk and add slowly to dry ingredients, stirring until smooth. On floured board knead until smooth; then roll ½ inch thick. Cut with biscuit cutter first dipped in flour. Crease each circle with back of knife one side of center. Butter small section and fold larger part well over small. Place far apart on greased pan. Allow to stand fifteen minutes in a warm place. Brush with melted butter and bake in hot oven, 425 degrees, for 15-20 minutes.

Submitted by Sister Mary Charissia Powers, SSND (deceased)

School Sisters of Notre Dame
Celebrating **175** *years*

Peanut Butter Balls

Makes 30 cookies

1 cup butter or margarine, room temperature
2 cups peanut butter
3½ cups powdered sugar
1 teaspoon vanilla

Mix all together. Chill till firm enough to handle. Roll into tablespoon-size balls and chill again until firm.

Dip:

1 (12-ounce) bag chocolate chips
1 square unsweetened chocolate
½ stick (about 2 ounces) food grade paraffin wax

Melt ingredients in a double boiler. Using a fork, dip balls into chocolate and pull out quickly when coated evenly. Place on wax paper to dry. Store in an air-tight container in refrigerator.

Submitted by Kathleen Storms, SSND from Mankato, MN

256

Peanut Butter Cookies

Makes 6 dozen cookies

1 cup shortening or butter, softened
1 cup white sugar
1 cup brown sugar
1 cup peanut butter
2 eggs
2½ cups all purpose flour
2 teaspoons baking soda
½ teaspoon salt

Mix all ingredients together. Drop by rounded spoonfuls onto ungreased cookie sheet. Bake at 350 degrees for 15 minutes or until edges are slightly brown.

257

Submitted by Dolorita Sierszynski, SSND from Mount Calvary, WI

Organic coffee
is grown without synthetic pesticides, herbicides,
or fertilizers under a canopy of shade trees,
protecting plants and soil and providing
winter habitat for migratory birds.

School Sisters of Notre Dame
Celebrating **175** *years*

Rhubarb Bread

....

Makes 4 loaves

2¾ **cups all-purpose flour**
1½ **cups brown sugar**, packed
1 **teaspoon baking soda**
1 **teaspoon salt**
1 **egg**
1 **cup buttermilk**
⅓ **cup cooking oil**
1 **teaspoon vanilla**
1 **cup fresh or frozen rhubarb**, finely chopped
8-12 **teaspoons butter or margarine**

258

Grease four small (6x3x2 inch) loaf pans. In a large mixing bowl, stir together the flour, sugar, baking soda and salt. In another bowl combine egg, buttermilk, cooking oil and vanilla. Stir into dry ingredients. Mix well. Fold rhubarb into batter. Pour batter into prepared pans. Spread on top of each loaf 2 or 3 teaspoons butter or margarine. Bake in a 350 degree oven for about 45-55 minutes until a wooden tooth pick inserted into the center of loaf comes out clean. Cool about 10 minutes in pan, and then remove from pan.

Submitted by Bernita Wasinger, SSND from Jefferson City, MO

Rhubarb Coffee Cake

Serves 10

Rhubarb is a spring gift to Minnesotans. This recipe is a fine way to begin the morning.

3 to 4 cups rhubarb
½ cup orange marmalade
1 egg
1 cup sugar
½ cup butter or margarine, softened
1 teaspoon vanilla
½ teaspoon salt
1 cup milk
3 teaspoons baking powder
2 cups flour

259

Cut and dice fresh rhubarb. Cover with boiling water and drain immediately. Stir in marmalade and set aside. Make cake batter using the rest of the ingredients, mixing them in the order given. Pour into a greased 9x13 inch pan. Spread rhubarb and marmalade mixture over the batter. Bake at 350 degrees for 40 minutes or until browned and rhubarb is done. Frost with powdered sugar, if desired. Very good without frosting.

Submitted by Kathleen Storms, SSND from Mankato, MN

COOKING *A Celebration of*
EARTH'S GIFTS

Rye Bread

Makes 2 loaves

2 cups rye flour
½ cup sugar
1 tablespoon salt
2 cups water, boiling
1 package yeast
½ cup water, warm
1 teaspoon sugar
2 heaping tablespoons shortening or margarine
¼ cup molasses
2½ tablespoons caraway seeds (optional)
4⅓ cups flour

260

Combine rye flour, sugar and salt. Add boiling water and beat.
Chill. Dissolve yeast in warm water and 1 teaspoon sugar. Stir into
rye flour mixture. Add shortening, molasses, caraway seeds and
enough flour to make a smooth dough. Knead for 10 minutes on
a lightly floured surface. Place in greased bowl. Turn to coat all
over with oil. Cover. Set in a warm place. Let rise until doubled.
Form into two loaves and place in greased bread pans. Cover
with clean towel. Let rise. Bake at 350 degrees for 50 minutes.
Remove from pans and cool on wire rack.

Submitted by Joan Bartosh, SSND from Rochester, MN

School Sisters of Notre Dame
Celebrating **175** *years*

Sandra's Sticky Buns

Makes 18

This is originally from Sandra Ann Weinke, SSND, presently in Nigeria.

1 (18-ounce) package frozen Parker House rolls
1 package butterscotch pudding mix, not instant
4 tablespoons (½ stick) butter or margarine
½ cup brown sugar
1 teaspoon ground cinnamon
½ cup pecans, chopped

Grease a bundt or round cake pan. Place frozen rolls in pan.
(They will rise so they need room.) Sprinkle the dry pudding mix
over the rolls. Melt the butter; add sugar and cinnamon and mix
well. Pour over the frozen rolls and pudding mix. Sprinkle with
the pecans. Cover with wax paper and a dish towel and let rise
overnight. Bake in the morning in a 350 degree oven for
25 minutes. Turn over onto a large plate and let it settle for a
minute before removing the pan. It is messy but so good.

261

Submitted by Jacqueline Buckley, SSND from Milwaukee, WI

Simple Sweet Cornbread

Makes 1 loaf

1¼ **cups flour**
¾ **cup cornmeal**
2 **teaspoons baking powder**
¼ **teaspoon salt**
2 **or 3 tablespoons butter,** softened (may substitute ¼ cup oil)
¼ **cup sugar**
1 **egg**
1 **cup milk**

262 Mix flour, cornmeal, baking powder and salt. Set aside. Cream together butter (or oil) and sugar with the back of a mixing spoon. Beat the egg into the butter and sugar mixture. (A wire whisk is best for this.) Gradually mix together the combined dry ingredients with the milk and the egg mixture alternating dry ingredients and egg mixture. Mix well after each addition. Lightly grease a regular bread loaf pan. Pre-heat the oven to 400 degrees. Pour batter into pan. Then whip or stir vigorously until the mixture is smooth. Bake for 35-40 minutes. Remove from the oven and immediately remove from the pan to cool. Allow to cool 5-10 minutes before slicing.

Submitted by Yvonne Conley, SSND from Milwaukee, WI

Sister Eugenia's Boston Brown Bread

Makes 3 loaves

When we were Novices, Sister Eugenia taught us how to bake this bread.

4 cups flour
1 cup whole wheat flour
1¼ teaspoons baking powder
1¼ teaspoons baking soda
1½ cups sugar (brown or white)
1 teaspoon salt
5 cups All-Bran
4 cups buttermilk
1¼ cups dark corn syrup
½ cup raisins

263

Stir together the flours, baking powder, baking soda, sugar and salt. Add the All-Bran, buttermilk and syrup. Mix well. Add the raisins. Pour into 3 well-greased loaf pans. Cover with aluminum foil in order to steam. Bake at 350 degrees for 1½ hours. Carefully remove immediately and cool.

Submitted by Edith Juergensmeyer, SSND from Jefferson City, MO

School Sisters of Notre Dame
Celebrating **175** *years*

Sliced Nut Cookies

Makes 16 dozen

Recipe can be cut in half.

1½ **cups butter or margarine,** softened
1 **cup white sugar**
2 **cups brown sugar**
3 **eggs**
½ **pound blanched almonds,** finely chopped
3½ **cups flour**
1 **teaspoon salt**
1 **teaspoon cinnamon**
1 **teaspoon baking soda**
Almonds, sliced

264

Cream the butter or margarine with the white sugar, then the brown sugar. Beat each egg one at a time into the creamed mixture. Add the blanched almonds. Sift together the flour, salt, cinnamon and baking soda, then fold into the butter mixture. Roll the dough into long rolls about 2 inches in diameter, wrap in waxed paper, and refrigerate overnight. To bake, cut slices about ¼ inch thick; put on cookie sheet, and place one thinly sliced almond in center of each cookie. Bake in moderate, 350 degrees, oven for 9-11 minutes. Check first cookie sheet for timing.

Icing:

Ice, if desired. Mix powdered sugar and water until the mixture reaches the consistency to thinly glaze each cookie.

Submitted by Susan Jordan, SSND from St. Louis, MO

Snow Drop Cookies

Makes 30 to 40 cookies

3 egg whites
½ cup sugar
⅛ teaspoon cream of tartar
½ to 1 cup chocolate chips, coconut, nuts or any kind of cereal.

Heat oven to 400 degrees. Beat the egg whites until stiff, gradually adding sugar while beating. Add the cream of tartar. Mixture should be stiff. Fold in choice of chocolate chips, coconut, etc. Drop by spoonfuls onto a lined or Teflon baking sheet. Put in oven, wait 8-10 minutes, then turn off oven. Allow oven to cool completely (or overnight) and remove cookies.

265

Submitted by Marie Angela Bayne, SSND from Key Biscayne, FL

Sweeten *foods with* **honey**
instead of refined sugar or corn syrup.

School Sisters of Notre Dame
Celebrating **175** *years*

Sugar Cookies

Makes 6½ dozen

1 cup powdered sugar
1 cup granulated sugar
1 cup margarine
1 cup cooking oil
2 eggs
1½ tablespoons vanilla
4¼ cups flour
½ teaspoon salt
1 tablespoon baking soda
1 tablespoon cream of tartar

Cream sugars and margarine. Add oil, eggs and vanilla. Beat well. Combine flour, salt, baking soda and cream of tartar. Add to first mixture. Chill. Form into balls and roll in granulated sugar. Bake on ungreased cookie sheet at 350 degrees. If balls are left whole, 12 to 15 minutes. If balls are flattened, 10 to12 minutes. They melt in your mouth.

Submitted by Regine Collins, SSND from Elm Grove, WI

Toffee Bars

Makes 16

12 whole graham crackers
½ cup butter
½ cup margarine
½ cup sugar
Almonds, pecans or English walnuts, chopped

Grease jelly roll pan. Break graham crackers apart and place on jelly roll pan, touching. Melt the butter and margarine. Add the sugar. Bring to boil and boil 2 minutes. Pour over graham crackers and spread with a spoon to cover entirely. Sprinkle with the nuts. Bake at 325 degrees for 12 minutes. Remove from oven immediately; place on wax paper, separate and cool.

267

Submitted by Odile Poliquin, SSND from St. Louis, MO

School Sisters of Notre Dame
Celebrating **175** *years*

Yeast Rolls/Bread

Makes 2 loaves

3 tablespoons yeast or 3 packages dry yeast
2 cups water, lukewarm
½ cup shortening
½ teaspoon salt
½ cup sugar
2 eggs, beaten
6 cups flour

268

Dissolve yeast in lukewarm water. Combine shortening, salt and sugar. Add the beaten egg. Stir in flour to make a soft dough. All ingredients are now mixed together. Let rise until double in size. Then make into loaves or rolls. Let it rise again. Bake in a 375 degree oven until brown.

Submitted in 1993 Leocadia Meyer, SSND from St. Louis, MO (deceased)

Welcome each other with a comfortable cup of tea. Catherine McCauley, RSM

School Sisters of Notre Dame
Celebrating **175** *years*

Yummy Graham Wafer Cookies

Makes 4 dozen balls

1½ squares semi-sweet chocolate
1 (14-ounce/300ml) can condensed milk
1 tablespoon butter or margarine
2 cups graham wafer cookie crumbs (36 singles crushed)
1 teaspoon vanilla
Medium sweet coconut or finely crushed nuts

Melt together chocolate, milk and butter. Mix in crumbs. Add
vanilla. Put in fridge to chill for a few hours. Form into small balls.
Roll in coconut.

269

Submitted by Joyce Lorentz, SSND from Regina, Saskatchewan, Canada

Zucchini Squares

Serves 8-10

8 cups zucchini, peeled and sliced like apples
⅔ cup lemon juice
1 cup sugar
½ teaspoon nutmeg
½ teaspoon cinnamon

Cook zucchini and lemon juice until tender. Add sugar and spices. Cool.

270

Crust:
1½ cups (3 sticks) margarine
4 cups flour
2 cups sugar
½ teaspoon cinnamon

Mix together. Press ½ of crust mixture in a 10x15 inch jelly roll pan. Bake at 350 degrees for 10 min. Pour cooled zucchini mixture over crust. Crumble rest of crust mixture over top. Sprinkle with ½ teaspoon cinnamon.   Bake at 350 degrees for 40 minutes. Cool. Cut into squares.

Submitted by Mary Beck, SSND from Mount Calvary, WI

DESSERTS & CANDY

271

from Mother Caroline's pen:

Eating candy during the instructions was universal. Our advice concerning the harm that can be done to teeth or stomach or blood went unheeded . . . Next, we placed a savings bank in the room for their donations to the poor.

At first, many pennies were put in because they were ashamed not to do so, but when they saw the fruits of their generosity in the form of new shoes or clothing on poor children, they gave willingly and with pleasure.

One result was that there was very little eating and chewing candy in class. The Letters of Mother Caroline Friess, School Sisters of Notre Dame, edited by Barbara Brumleve, SSND, p.33

Angel Food Pineapple Cake

Serves 12

1 one-step Angel food cake mix
1 (20-ounce) can crushed pineapple with juice
Whipped topping
Chocolate syrup (optional)
Strawberries (optional)

Mix cake mix and pineapple together. Bake in a prepared
9x11 inch pan at 350 degrees for about 40 minutes. Cool.
Before serving, frost with whipped topping. Drizzle chocolate
syrup or a few strawberries on top.

Submitted by Marguerite Churilla, SSND from St. Cloud, MN

Apple Bread Pudding

Serves 6

2 eggs, beaten
⅓ **cup sugar**
½ **teaspoon cinnamon**
⅛ **teaspoon salt**
2 cups stale bread cubes
1 cup apples, pared, thinly-sliced
2 cups milk

In greased 1 quart baking dish, mix eggs, sugar, cinnamon and salt. Add bread, apples and milk. Stir gently and let set for 5 minutes. Bake uncovered at 350 degrees for 45-55 minutes or until knife inserted into center comes out clean. Let stand 15 minutes before serving. Serve with ice cream or whipped topping.

275

Submitted by Ruth Speh, SSND from St. Louis, MO (deceased)

Apple Crisp

Serves 6-8

A favorite of my whole family.

5-6 cups apples, pared and sliced
1 cup sifted flour
½ to 1 cup sugar, according to desired taste
1 teaspoon baking powder
¾ teaspoon salt
1 egg, unbeaten
⅓ cup margarine, melted
½ teaspoon cinnamon

276

Place apples in a greased 6x10 inch baking dish. Mix together flour, sugar, baking powder, salt and egg with fork until crumbly. Sprinkle mixture over apples; then pour melted margarine over all. Sprinkle with cinnamon. Bake uncovered 30-40 minutes at 350 degrees. Serve warm with whipped topping or ice cream.

Submitted by Charlene Zeisset, SSND from St. Louis, MO

Apple Fritters

Serves 6

2+ apples
1 cup flour, sifted
1¼ teaspoons baking powder
¼ teaspoon salt
1 egg beaten
⅓ cup milk
Oil for frying

Peel apples and core, then slice but not too thin. Mix the rest of ingredients to form a batter. Dip the apple slices in batter. Fry in hot oil until golden brown, remove and sprinkle with powdered sugar.

277

Submitted in 1993 by Agnes Marie Schulte, SSND from Dallas, TX (deceased)

Food reveals
our connection to Earth.
*Each bite contains the life
of the sun and Earth.*

We can see and taste the whole universe
in a piece of bread!

Thich Nhat Hanh

School Sisters of Notre Dame
Celebrating **175** *years*

Berliner Pfannkuchen

Makes 24

The German word "Berliner" can either denote one who is a citizen of Berlin or a particular kind of jelly-filled donut. Here we have the donut.

4 cups flour
⅓ cup barm (yeast) or 1 pack dry yeast and
    ½ cup lukewarm water
6 tablespoons (¾ stick) butter, softened
⅓ cup sugar
2 yolks and 2 eggs
2 tablespoons rum
1 lemon peel, grated
Apricot jam

278

Make a tender barm-dough by mixing together all ingredients except jam. Place in greased bowl, cover and let it rise in a warm place until doubled. Place on a floured board, knead and roll out dough until it is as thick as your little finger. Mark circles on half the dough with a glass. Put some jam in the middle of the circles. Gently place the other half of the dough on top so that the jam dollops are easy to see and not spread out. Use a glass to cut out the donuts. Lightly press the edges to seal the top and bottom. Cover with a shawl and let them rise in a warm place until large.

Heat the fat to 180 degrees Celsius or 370 degrees Fahrenheit. Bake the doughnuts on the first side in a covered pot (about 5 minutes) and the second side uncovered (about 10 minutes). Use enough oil so that the doughnuts can swim. Then let the oil drain off and sprinkle the doughnuts with fine sugar.

Submitted in 1991 by Maria Romana Klina, SSND from Berlin, Germany

School Sisters of Notre Dame
Celebrating **175** *years*

Betty Lee's Pineapple Bake

Serves 9

Delicious served hot with ham. Served cold, it is a tempting dessert.

3 eggs
½ cup sugar
4 tablespoons butter or margarine, melted
1 (20-ounce) can crushed pineapple with juice
5 slices fresh bread, cut in one inch cubes, no crusts

Beat eggs and sugar together. Add butter and pineapple with juice. Add bread cubes. Mix well but gently. Bake uncovered in greased 8X8 inch casserole for 50 minutes at 350 degrees.

279

Submitted by Betty Sweeney, SSND Associate from Baltimore, MD

Bride's Dessert

Serves 12

1 (20-ounce) can crushed pineapple with juice
1 (20-ounce) can pie filling
1 box 2-layer cake mix
½ cup (1 stick) butter

Grease an oblong 9x13 inch Pyrex pan. Spread the pineapple in it. Over this evenly spread the can of pie filling. Sprinkle the cake mix over the mixture. Dot butter on top. Bake at 350 degrees for 1 hour. Cool and serve plain or with ice cream.

280   Submitted by Rita Mary Schweihs, SSND from Homer Glen, IL

Candied Peanuts

Makes 4 cups

A favorite recipe that I used in Africa and continue to use here.

4 cups raw peanuts with skins on (Spanish Peanuts are great)
2 cups sugar
1 cup water
1 teaspoon red food color

Combine all ingredients in a sauce pan. Cook over medium heat, stirring constantly, until all the water is absorbed and the sugar coats the peanuts. Spread peanuts on a baking sheet and bake in a 250 degree oven for one hour. Stir every 15 minutes. Cool and store in an air-tight container.

281

Submitted by Frances Eveler, SSND from St. Louis, MO

Caramels

Makes about 4 pounds of caramels

1 cup butter or margarine
2 cups white sugar
2 cups white syrup
1 (14-ounce) can sweetened condensed milk
1 teaspoon vanilla
1 cup nuts (optional)

282

Put margarine, sugar, syrup and half of milk in a Dutch-oven. Bring to boiling on medium heat stirring very frequently. Add the rest of the milk and stir constantly. Cook to about 245 degrees on a candy thermometer. Take off heat and add vanilla and nuts.

Pour into a well-buttered jelly-roll pan, a cookie sheet with an edge, or a cake pan to cool. Cut into squares and store in a lightly covered container. Do not refrigerate or freeze.

Submitted by Carol Marie Hemish, SSND from Buffalo, MN

Cheese Clods

2 pounds white cheese (cottage cheese)
3 eggs
⅔ cup flour
⅔ cup sugar
⅓ cup grits
1 tablespoon pudding powder
Salt
Vanilla
Orange peel, grated

Put the white cheese through a strainer; mix in the eggs and the other ingredients till the dough is smooth. Spoon clods into boiling salt water. Test one clod first. If it is too soft add some grits to the dough. When the clods begin to boil, let them stay in for about 10 minutes. When they swim on the surface, they are done. Serve them with brown sugar, butter and cinnamon.

283

Submitted in 1991 by Maria Romana Klina, SSND from Berlin, Germany

Chocolate Cake

Serves 12-16

1½ cups cake flour
1 teaspoon salt
1½ teaspoons baking soda
½ cup cocoa
⅔ cup oil
1 cup buttermilk
1 teaspoon vanilla
2 eggs
1¼ cups sugar

284

Stir together the flour, salt, baking soda and cocoa. Add the oil, buttermilk and vanilla. Beat until it forms a very smooth batter. In a separate bowl, beat the eggs until thick and foamy. Gradually add the sugar and continue beating until blended. Fold the sugar and egg mixture into batter and pour into two 8 inch round oiled and floured cake pans. Bake at 350 degrees for 30-35 minutes.

White Whipped Frosting:

1 cup milk
2 tablespoons cornstarch
1 cup sugar

1 cup butter, softened
1 teaspoon vanilla

Combine milk and cornstarch and cook until thick. Then allow to cool. In a mixing bowl beat the sugar, butter and vanilla. Beat until snowy white, 5-10 minutes. Fold in cooled milk mixture and beat 15 minutes or until whipped.

Submitted by Florence Stroeder, SSND from Waterdown, Ontario, Canada

School Sisters of Notre Dame
Celebrating **175** *years*

Chocolate Cherry Cake

Serves 15

This recipe was a 3rd place winner in a recipe contest.

1 package 2-layer fudge cake mix
1 (21-ounce) can cherry pie filling
2 tablespoons water
2 eggs, beaten
1 teaspoon almond extract

Grease and flour a 9X13 inch pan. Preheat oven to 350 degrees. Combine all ingredients in large mixing bowl. Stir by hand until well blended. Spread in prepared pan. Bake for 35 to 40 minutes or until top of cake springs back to light touch. Remove from oven and cool slightly. Frost with Chocolate Icing.

285

Chocolate Icing:
1 cup granulated sugar
5 tablespoons butter or margarine
¼ cup milk
1 cup chocolate chips

In a sauce pan, combine sugar, butter or margarine and milk. Bring to a boil over medium heat and boil for 1 minute. Remove from heat and stir in chocolate chips. Stir until smooth and spread over slightly cooled cake.

Submitted by M. Clared Coyne, SSND from Chatawa, MS

School Sisters of Notre Dame
Celebrating **175** *years*

Chocolate Mint Sundaes

Serves 4

Keep ice cream and a bag of peppermint patties in the freezer to create this quick dessert.

12 (0.25-ounce) peppermint patties
2 tablespoons milk
Vanilla ice cream

Place peppermint patties and milk in a small microwave-safe glass bowl. Cover and microwave at HIGH one minute or until patties melt, stirring every 15 seconds.
Serve over ice cream.

Submitted by Jovann Irrgang, SSND from Dallas, TX

286

Coconut Cake

Serves 12

2 cups sugar
1 cup oil
5 eggs
2 cups flour
½ teaspoon salt
1½ teaspoons baking powder
½ cup milk
1 teaspoon vanilla
1 cup angel flake coconut
1 teaspoon coconut flavoring

287

Mix sugar and oil. Add eggs one at a time. Beat well. Mix flour, salt and baking powder. Add to first mixture with milk and vanilla, coconut, and coconut flavoring. Grease and flour tube pan. Pour in batter. Bake at 325 degrees for 1 hour.

Glaze:
1 cup sugar
½ cup water
1 teaspoon coconut flavoring

Boil for 1 minute. Poke holes into cake with a straw and pour mixture over cake. Let stand for one hour.

Submitted in 1993 by Dorothy Malone, SSND from Cookeysville, MO

Coconut-Almond Dessert

Serves 12

½ **cup butter or margarine,** melted
1 **cup flour**
1¼ **cups flaked coconut**
¼ **cup brown sugar,** packed
1 **package slivered almonds**
2 **(4-serving size) packages instant vanilla pudding**
2⅔ **cups milk,** cold
1 **(8-ounce) container whipped topping**

288

Combine the first five ingredients and press lightly into a greased 9x13 inch baking dish. Bake at 350 for 25-30 minutes or until golden brown, stirring every 10 minutes to form crumbs. Let mixture cool and then divide in half. Press half into the same baking dish. In a mixing bowl, beat pudding mixes and milk. Fold in whipped topping. Spread over crust. Top with remaining crumb mixture. Cover and refrigerate overnight. Top with strawberries or other fruit if desired.

Submitted by Paulette Zimmerman, SSND from St. Louis, MO

Crummy Pie

Serves 8-10

1 (9-inch) pie crust
1 cup walnuts, chopped medium fine
1 cup sugar, divided
½ cup fine soda cracker crumbs (14-16 crackers)
¼ teaspoon baking soda
3 eggs, separated
¼ teaspoon salt
¼ cup lemon juice
1 teaspoon lemon rind, grated
1 teaspoon vanilla
Whipped cream or whipped topping

289

Roll and shape pie crust making a high fluted edge. Bake at 450 degrees about 7 minutes or just until crust starts to turn brown. Mix walnuts and ½ cup sugar, cracker crumbs and soda. Set aside. Beat egg whites with salt until stiff, but not dry. Beat egg yolks until thick, then beat in remaining ½ cup sugar. Stir in lemon juice, rind, and vanilla. Fold together whites, walnut mixture and yolks just until well blended. Pour into crust. Bake at 350 degrees about 35 minutes or until well browned. Cool and serve with whipped cream or whipped topping.

Submitted by Sharon Rempe, SSND from St. Louis, MO

Czech Apple Strudel

Serves 24

This is a Czech Christmas specialty dough.

½ **cup butter or margarine**
½ **cup hot water**
1 egg
¼ **teaspoon salt**
2 cups flour

Melt butter in hot water, add egg and salt. Add flour to make soft dough. Place dough in warm bowl and cover. Let stand in warm place 10 minutes or longer. Divide into 2 parts. On a floured towel, stretch dough out paper thin.

290

Filling:
1 cup fine bread crumbs
½ **cup coconut**
1 cup sugar
½ **cup nuts,** chopped
½ **cup raisins**
2 cups apples, finely chopped
1 teaspoon cinnamon

Mix together. Spread on dough. Roll up, using towel to help**.**

(Continued on next page)

Glaze:

½ **cup cream**
¼ **cup sugar**

Before baking, brush with a glaze of cream and sugar. Bake at 350 for 45 minutes. After it has been in the oven for 30 minutes, brush again with the glaze. Brush again after removing from oven.

Submitted by Barbara Simek, SSND from Prior Lake, MN

....

In Thanksgiving For All That Is

by Barb Zurine, SSND

Resplendent sunrise
calling forth the new day
awakening autumn
to brilliant earthen shades,
lemon-drop mums
fields of golden wheat
vines of orange bittersweet,
speckled colored leaves
dancing on the wind
get togethers
with family and friends,
asking blessings
on our homeland and all nations
reverencing life
in all of creation.
Working for justice
and universal peace
cherishing our God-given gift
to be free.
Give us grateful hearts, Lord
help us to plant the seed
so we can become
the change we want to see.

291

copyright - 2002

School Sisters of Notre Dame
Celebrating **175** *years*

Derby Pie

Serves 8-10

This recipe won first place and was a Grand Prize Winner in a recipe contest.

½ **cup (1 stick) butter,** melted
1 **cup sugar**
1 **cup white corn syrup**
4 **eggs**
1 **tablespoon bourbon**
1 **cup nuts**
½ **cup chocolate chips**
1 **unbaked pie shell**
Whipped topping (optional)

292

Mix ingredients and pour into pie shell. Bake for 45 minutes at 350 degrees. Garnish with whipped cream or whipped topping if desired.

Submitted by M. Clared Coyne, SSND from Chatawa, MS

Fasnacht Küchli

Serves 18-22

This is from my mom and a favorite for Mardi Gras.

1 egg
¼ teaspoon salt
2 tablespoons salad oil
¼ cup milk
1½ cups all purpose flour
1 tablespoon sugar
Oil
Granulated sugar

293

Place egg in mixing bowl, add salt, salad oil and milk. Mix well. Sift together flour and sugar and mix into liquid. When dough becomes too thick to stir with spoon, place on floured board and knead in balance of flour. Roll out like pie dough until about 16 inches in diameter. Cut into four-inch squares. Roll each square paper thin. Fry in deep hot fat using two forks to hold dough in shape. Fry until light brown. Place on absorbent paper and sprinkle generously with granulated sugar while hot.

Submitted by Charlene Zeisset, SSND from St. Louis, MO

Fastest Fudge

Makes 64 small pieces

2 cups milk chocolate chips
1 cup semi-sweet chocolate chips
1 (14-ounce) can sweetened condensed milk
1 teaspoon vanilla
Nuts (optional)

Melt the chips in a double boiler or in a microwave at half power. If you use the microwave, check it every 30 seconds. Stir when all are melted and shiny. Add the milk and vanilla; stir well. Finally add nuts. Spread in an 8X8 inch or 9X9 inch pan lined with waxed paper. Cool and cut into the size desired. Store in the refrigerator in a tightly closed container.

294

Submitted by Carol Marie Hemish, SSND from Buffalo, MN

Fried Pineapple

Serves 4

2 tablespoons flour
1 egg, beaten
Pinch salt
4 slices fresh pineapple
Butter or margarine
Cinnamon
Sugar

Mix flour, egg and salt to make a batter. Dip slices of pineapple into the mixture. In a frying pan, brown battered slices in butter on both sides. Drain and sprinkle with a mixture of cinnamon and sugar.

295

Submitted by Mary Kerber, SSND in Nairobi, Kenya

Fruit Pizza

Serves 12

Bottom layer:
1 cup margarine, softened
¾ cup granulated sugar
¾ cup brown sugar, packed
1 teaspoon vanilla
2 eggs
2¼ cups all-purpose flour, unsifted
1 teaspoon baking soda
½ teaspoon salt

296

Cream together margarine, sugar, brown sugar and vanilla. Add eggs. Beat well. Combine flour, baking soda and salt. Gradually beat into creamed mixture. Spread dough in a pizza pan. Bake 12 minutes at 350 degrees. Cool.

Second layer:
1 (8-ounce) package cream cheese
1 (7½-ounce) jar marshmallow cream
2 tablespoons brown sugar
Orange or lemon juice

Stir together the cream cheese, marshmallow cream and brown sugar. Add just enough orange or lemon juice to thin so it spreads easily. Spread on top of cooled first layer.

(Continued on next page)

Third layer:
Arrange fruit of all kinds on top of second layer about 30-45 minutes before serving. Suggestions include: **sliced bananas, strawberries, blueberries, pineapple, kiwi, peaches, raspberries, etc.**

Submitted in 1992 by Joan Bartosh, SSND from Rochester, MN

....

Join a CSA *(Community Supported Agriculture).*

A CSA is a partnership of mutual commitment between a farm and a community of supporters, who purchase harvest "shares" in the farm.

297

Each week the supporters receive whatever is ripe. They also may be asked to participate in the harvesting as well as enjoy seasonal festivals.

Most CSAs offer organic produce with some meat, eggs, dairy products, honey, bread and flowers.

The amount of food and length of commitment varies from farm to farm, so explore local options to find one that fits your interests.

Churches can be great drop-off points for customers participating in a CSA.

To find a CSA near you go to: http://www.localharvest.org/csa/

School Sisters of Notre Dame
Celebrating **175** *years*

Fruity Ice

Serves 24

Caution! When eating Fruity Ice, gently dig your fork into it. A gentleman guest at our convent dug his fork into it like you would a pitch fork into a pile of hay! His piece of fruity ice flipped up and into his water.

2 cups sugar
1 cup water

Bring water and sugar to a boil and cool.

298

1 large can crushed pineapple, undrained
1 carton frozen strawberries, undrained
3 bananas, sliced
1 large can apricots, drained

Mix fruit together in a 9x13 inch pan. Pour sugar water over fruit and place in freezer. Cut in squares and serve directly from freezer to table.

Submitted by Marjorie Rosenau, SSND from St. Paul, MN

Harvey Wallbanger Cake

Serves 12-16

1 package yellow 2-layer cake mix (do not use mix with oil already added)
1 (4-serving size) package instant vanilla pudding
4 eggs
2 ounces each of vodka and any "golden" Italian liqueur
6 ounces orange juice
8 ounces oil

Mix all ingredients and beat at medium speed for 4 minutes. Bake at 350 degrees for 45 minutes. If cake springs back when tested with a straw, it is done. Cool on wire rack for 15 minutes.

299

Submitted by Betty Sweeney, SSND Associate from Baltimore, MD

Heavenly Hash

Serves 27

2 cups chocolate chips
2 tablespoons margarine
1 (14-ounce) can condensed milk
2 or more cups miniature marshmallows
1 cup nuts, chopped

Melt chocolate chips, margarine, and milk in a double boiler.
Mix marshmallows and nuts in a large mixing bowl. Pour melted
chocolate mixture over marshmallows and nuts. Stir until covered
with chocolate. Spread in a 9X13 inch pan lined with wax paper.
Chill for 2 to 3 hours. Cut in desired sizes.

300

Submitted by Odile Poliquin, SSND from St. Louis, MO

Jiffy Rhubarb Crisp

Serves 9

4 cups rhubarb, diced
1 cup sugar
1 (4-serving size) package strawberry or raspberry jello (sugar free can be used)
1 package Jiffy white cake mix (1-layer cake mix)
¼ cup margarine, melted
Whipped topping or ice cream

Place rhubarb in a 9 inch square baking pan. Sprinkle sugar over rhubarb. Sprinkle jello directly from package over the sugar. **301** Pour the cake mix directly from the package over the jello. Dribble the margarine over the dry cake layer. Bake at 350 degrees for 25-30 minutes. Serve with whipped topping or ice cream.

Submitted by Joan Bartosh, SSND from Rochester, MN

Kolacky (Czech Pastry)
....

Makes 5 dozen

This recipe appeared in the Notre Dame Centenary Cookbook put together by our wonderful "cook" Sisters in 1947.

½ **pound butter or Crisco,** softened
1 **cup sugar**
3 **egg yolks**
2 **yeast cakes or two packages active dry yeast**
2 **cups milk,** scalded and cooled
8 **cups of flour**
A **little lemon rind**

302

Cream the butter, sugar and yolks. Add yeast which has been dissolved in a little warm water. Add milk and flour alternately. Add lemon rind. Cover and let rise. After the dough is doubled in bulk, it is ready to use.

Filling for the Kolacky:
1 **cup poppy seeds,** ground
½ **cup raisins**
Boil poppy seeds in water or milk and sweeten with honey or sugar. *Here are two ways to make the Kolacky: On a lightly floured surface roll the dough to ½ inch thickness and cut into 3 inch rounds. Place on greased baking sheets, cover and let rise until double. Press in center and fill with filling. Bake at 400 degrees for 15 minutes. Alternatively, sprinkle counter with flour and powdered sugar, roll the dough to ½ inch or ¼ inch thickness, cut into 3 inch squares, place filling in the center, pinch together the corners of the dough. Bake at 350 for 20 minutes.*
Submitted by Sister M. Martina, SSND from Silverlake, MN

School Sisters *of* Notre Dame
Celebrating **175** *years*

Lemon Cake With Diet Ski Soda

Serves 12

1 (2-layer) lemon cake mix
1 diet ski soda or other citrus soda

Mix together and bake according to directions given on cake box. The soda takes the place of the liquids called for in the mix directions.

Icing for Cake:
1 tub fat free whipped topping
1 small package diet lemon jello, powder
Mix together and ice cake. **303**

Variations:
White cake mix with diet orange soda
Chocolate cake mix with diet black cherry soda

Submitted by Tessie Markus, SSND from Belleville, IL

Mary's Favorite Apple Upside Down Cake

Serves 15

¼ cup margarine
¼ cup brown sugar
½ cup water
8-10 apples, peeled, cored and cut into wedges about ½ inch thick at widest part
¼ cup white sugar
1 teaspoon cinnamon
¼ teaspoon nutmeg
4 eggs, separated
1 cup sugar
1½ cups all-purpose flour
1 teaspoon baking powder
¼ teaspoon salt
½ cup boiling water
1 teaspoon vanilla or lemon juice
¼ teaspoon cream of tartar

304

Melt margarine in a 9x13 inch pan. Sprinkle with brown sugar and water. Line pan with apples in rows. Mix together white sugar, cinnamon and nutmeg. Sprinkle over apples.

For batter, separate eggs. Beat the yolks, adding sugar. Sift together flour, baking powder and salt. Add to yolk mixture alternating with boiling water. Add vanilla or lemon juice. Beat egg whites with cream of tartar until stiff. Fold into batter and pour over apples.

(continued on next page)

Bake at 350 degrees 40-50 minutes or until toothpick comes out clean. Immediately run knife around edges of pan and invert onto serving tray. Gently remove pan. If any apples stick to the bottom replace them into the empty spaces.

Submitted by Mary Beck, SSND from Mount Calvary, WI

Enjoy *a cup of coffee, tea or cocoa* **with this cake.**

Equal Exchange, *a worker-owned co-op* *dedicated to* ***fair trade*** *offers all three.*

FAIR TRADE certified means that the farmers received a fair price for the coffee, which is generally certified organic and shade-grown. Look for this internationally recognized,

independently monitored label on tea, chocolate, and cocoa.

305

Learn More at:
www.equalexchange.com
www.TransFairUSA.org
www.tenthousandvillages.ca
www.oxfam.org

School Sisters of Notre Dame
Celebrating **175** *years*

Midnight Bliss Cake

Serves 10-12

This is a chocolate lover's delight! It may be garnished with fresh raspberries or your favorite ice cream.

1 package 2-layer chocolate cake mix
1 (4 serving size) package chocolate instant pudding
½ cup General Foods International Coffee, any flavor
4 eggs
1 cup sour cream
½ cup oil
½ cup water
1 package of 8 squares semi-sweet baking chocolate, chopped

306

Beat all ingredients, except the chopped chocolate in a large bowl with an electric mixer on low speed just until moistened, scraping side of bowl often. Beat on medium speed 2 minutes or until well blended. Stir in chopped chocolate. Spoon batter into lightly greased and floured 12-cup fluted tube pan or 10 inch tube pan.

Bake at 350 degrees for 50 to 60 minutes or until toothpick inserted near center comes out clean. Cool in pan 10 minutes on wire rack. Loosen cake from side of pan with spatula or knife. Invert cake onto rack and gently remove pan. Cool cake completely on wire rack. Place on serving plate and sprinkle with powdered sugar and drizzle with warm fudge ice cream topping.
Suggested substitute: 2 tablespoons instant coffee for the ½ cup General Foods International Coffee

Submitted by Cheryl Marie Wagner, SSND from Mankato, MN

School Sisters of Notre Dame
Celebrating **175** *years*

Miniature Cheese Cakes

Serves 12

12 Vanilla wafers
2 (8-ounce) packages cream cheese
2 eggs
¾ cup sugar
1 tablespoon lemon juice
1 (21-ounce) can pie filling (cherry, blueberry, etc.)
Paper baking cups (choose a size suitable to the size
of vanillla wafer)

Place paper baking cups in muffin tins. Place vanilla wafer in
each cup. Combine cream cheese, eggs, sugar and lemon
juice. Beat well. Fill cups ⅔ full and bake at 375 degrees for
15 minutes. Cool and top with pie filling.

307

Submitted in 1993 by Marie Torno, SSND from Chatawa, MS

Molasses Puffs Candy

Serves 6-8

1 cup dark Karo syrup / molasses
1 cup white sugar
1 tablespoon white vinegar
3½ teaspoons baking soda

In a heavy sauce pan, combine syrup, sugar and vinegar. Stir over medium heat until sugar is dissolved. Cook without stirring until candy thermometer registers 300 degrees. Remove from heat and add baking soda, stirring rapidly. Pour immediately into 9X9 inch lightly buttered pan. Avoid spreading. When cool, break into pieces. Makes about a pound. If desired, dip into melted chocolate. Store in a cool place.

Submitted by Maureen Brinker, SSND from St. Louis, MO

308

Mom's Dark Christmas Cake

Serves 75-80 small pieces

This recipe can be halved or quartered without changing the goodness. Adjust baking time accordingly.

1 cup walnuts, brazil nuts, hazel nuts, pecans
2 cups dates, cut up
2 cups raisins
1 cup each red and green candied cherries
2 cups mixed peel
8 cups pineapple tidbits, drained
1 wine glass (4-ounces) of whiskey
or
1 cup cherry brandy
2 cups flour
5 eggs
½ pound butter
1½ cups brown sugar
1 pinch each of cinnamon, cloves, nutmeg
½ cup corn syrup
1 teaspoon baking soda in ¼ cup hot water
2 cups large gum drops (not small baking gumdrops)
1 pinch salt

309

Mix all fruits and nuts together. Pour on cherry brandy and ¼ cup flour. Mix and let stand for several hours. Beat eggs, butter and brown sugar. Add remainder of ingredients; mix and then add this mixture to fruit and nut mixture.

Line 2 large baking tins with brown paper bag or parchment
(Continued on next page)

paper and grease. My mother used her rectangular roasting pan. Pour batter into tins and cover with tin foil. Heat oven at 200 degrees and bake for about four hours, or until toothpick comes out clean.

When cakes are cooled, cut into smaller loaf-size slabs. Soak cotton cloths in cherry brandy and wrap slab with moistened cloth. Pack in airtight container and keep in fridge or cool pantry. Every few days make sure cloths are moist. If not, change cloths with freshly moistened ones. Always good, but best after 3-4 weeks. Freezes well, if it lasts that long.

Submitted by Joyce Lorentz, SSND from Regina, Saskatchewan, Canada

Creator God

by Mary Gilda Sturino, SSND

Thank you
For the goodness of the earth
Which
Supports me
Surrounds me with beauty
Supplies me with food
And is a
Source of my healing.

New York Chunky Apple Sauce

Serves 12

New York State is famous for its numerous apple orchards. Many of us incorporate these apples into our meals. This helps our local farmers to flourish and encourages the food markets to sell local produce.

2 – 3 pounds of New York Apples
Cinnamon or nutmeg or both
Water or apple cider

Cut each apple into 4 pieces. Core and peel, leaving skin on some. Boil about 2 or 3 inches water or cider. Add cinnamon or nutmeg to taste. Add apples, a few at a time, and stir until all apples are in pot. Stir frequently. Cook about 15 minutes. When apples are soft and chunky, remove from pot. Cool and enjoy.

311

Submitted by Mariella McMillan, SSND from Rochester, NY

Nun Left...Burnt Almond

Makes 20-25 pieces

This candy is actually called Burnt Almond, but friends in northern Ontario renamed it NUNFOOD, and then NUNLEFT when it kept disappearing.

½ pound butter (1 cup)
1 cup white sugar
1½ cups slivered almonds
1 cup chocolate chips, or to taste

312

In saucepan melt butter on medium high. Add sugar and almonds. Stir constantly for 8-10 minutes, until consistency is creamy caramel and mixture begins to smoke. Pour and spread on ungreased cookie sheet. Sprinkle chocolate chips over it. Let sit until chocolate has melted and then spread it out with a knife. Let cool at least 3 hours or overnight. Break into pieces. Enjoy.

Submitted by Maureen McGoey, SSND from Rome, Italy

Nut Crisps

Serves 25

*This is a favourite recipe. Easy to make and first to be eaten. It came from
a very good friend who was also taught by the SSNDs.*

Graham crackers
1 cup butter or margarine
1 cup brown sugar
1 cup broken nuts – pecans or walnuts

Place crackers in a single layer in a 9x13 inch pan. Break some if
needed. Cook butter, brown sugar and nuts over medium heat.
Bring to boil. Spoon this mixture over the graham crackers and
bake at 350 for 10 minutes. Cut into squares when cooled a bit.
Then cool completely in pan.

313

Submitted by Theresa Harvey, SSND Associate from Hamilton, Ontario, Canada

Nuts And Bolts

Serves 60

1 box Cheerios (about 12 cups)
1 box Shreddies or other wheat squares cereal (about 12 cups)
½ package thin pretzel sticks (about 4 cups)
2 cups peanuts
1 cup margarine, melted
2 teaspoons seasoned salt
2 tablespoons worcestershire sauce
1 teaspoon garlic salt
1 teaspoon onion powder

314

Combine the Cheerios, Shreddies, peanuts and pretzels in a large bowl. In a saucepan, melt margarine. Add next 4 ingredients. When well mixed add to cereal mixture. Stir well. Bake in a 250 degree oven uncovered for 1½ hours. Stir every 20 minutes. Cool. Store in air-tight containers.

Submitted by Dianne Poitras, SSND Associate from Regina, Saskatchewan, Canada

One-Two-Three-Four Cake

Serves 12-16

1 cup butter or margarine, softened
2 cups sugar
3 cups all-purpose flour
4 eggs, separated
1 teaspoon salt
3 teaspoons baking powder
1 cup milk
1 teaspoon vanilla extract

Beat the butter and sugar until very light and creamy. Beat egg yolks and add. Sift flour twice with salt and baking powder. Add to creamed mixture alternately with milk, a little at a time. Add vanilla. Beat egg whites and fold into batter.

315

Pour batter into 3 greased, 9 inch layer pans. Bake at 350 degrees for 30 minutes. Cover with your favorite frosting.

Submitted in 1993 by Marie Torno, SSND from Chatawa, MS

School Sisters of Notre Dame
Celebrating **175** *years*

Orange Kiss Me Cake

Serves 12-16

1 cup sugar
½ cup margarine
2 eggs, well-beaten
¾ cup buttermilk
1 tablespoon orange rind, grated
½ cup nuts, finely chopped
1 teaspoon baking soda
2 cups flour

Mix in order and bake in greased tube pan at 350 degrees for 1 hour.

316

Filling:
1 cup orange juice
1 cup sugar
1 tablespoon orange rind

Boil a few minutes. Pour over cake while cake is hot. Keep pouring over the cake until it all soaks into the cake.

Submitted in 1993 by Leocadia Meyer, SSND from St. Louis, MO (deceased)

Our Mom's Rhubarb Custard Pie

Serves 10

*Our mom always put brown sugar over the rhubarb in the crust, but we
prefer to mix brown sugar with the eggs we pour over the rhubarb mixture.*

9-inch pie crust
4 cups rhubarb, chopped
1½ cups brown sugar, packed
1 teaspoon cinnamon
¼ to ½ teaspoon nutmeg
4-5 eggs
1 tablespoon tapioca
Small pieces margarine

317

Prepare crust for a deep 9-inch pie tin. Fill pie crust with rhubarb.
Mix brown sugar, cinnamon and nutmeg and pour into crust.
Beat eggs lightly with a fork. Add tapioca for thickening. Pour
eggs over rhubarb mixture. Put small pieces of margarine over
top. Bake at 350 degrees for 50 minutes and 450 degrees for
10 more minutes until crust is brown and pie is done.

Submitted by Alice Giere, SSND from Elm Grove, WI and Joan Frances
Giere, SSND from Detroit, MI

Perfect Pumpkin Pie

Serves 6-8

Can be made without crust as a custard.

2 cups pumpkin
1 (14-ounce) can sweetened condensed milk
2 eggs
1 teaspoon ground cinnamon
½ teaspoon ground ginger
½ teaspoon ground nutmeg
½ teaspoon vanilla
½ teaspoon salt
9-inch unbaked pie crust

318

Preheat oven to 425 degrees. Whisk pumpkin, milk, eggs, spices, vanilla and salt in medium bowl until smooth. Pour into crust. Bake 15 minutes. Reduce oven to 350 degrees and continue baking 35 to 40 minutes or until knife inserted comes out clean. Store leftovers in the refrigerator.

Submitted by Rita Marie Schneider, SSND from Mankato, MN

Pie Crust

Makes 2 or 1 with top crust

3 cups flour
1 teaspoon salt
1¼ cups shortening
1 egg
1 tablespoon vinegar
4 tablespoons water, cold

Mix the flour, salt and shortening together. Add the egg, vinegar and water. Press together into a ball. Divide into two pieces. Roll out each piece and put one piece into a pie pan. Put in a filling, put the other piece on top and bake.

319

Submitted by Odile Poliquin, SSND from St. Louis, MO

Pineapple Upside-down Cakes

Serves 12

1 (20-ounce) can pineapple slices, retain juice
¼ cup margarine, melted
¾ cup brown sugar
Yellow 1-layer cake mix

Mix margarine and brown sugar. Grease large muffin tins, put some margarine and brown sugar mixture into each tin. Place a pineapple slice on top of mixture. You may need to cut them to make them fit.

320 Prepare a yellow cake mix as directed on package using pineapple juice in place of water. Pour batter evenly into each cup. Use rest of batter to make plain cupcakes. Bake at 350 degrees for 20-25 minutes. Cool and invert onto serving plate. Place a red cherry in center. Optional: Spray whipped topping around bottom.

Submitted by Marguerite Churilla, SSND from St. Cloud, MN

Prune Cake

Serves 18

2 cups flour
1½ cups sugar
1 teaspoon baking soda
1 teaspoon salt
1 teaspoon allspice
1 teaspoon nutmeg
1 teaspoon cinnamon
1 cup vegetable oil
1 cup nuts or raisins
1 cup buttermilk
1 cup prunes, mashed
3 eggs
1 teaspoon vanilla

321

Sift together flour, sugar, baking soda, salt and spices. Add rest of ingredients. Mix until smooth. Pour into greased 9X13 inch pan. Bake at 300 degrees for 1 hour.

Sauce:
Prepare in the last 10 minutes before the cake is finished baking.
½ cup butter or margarine
⅓ teaspoon baking soda
1 tablespoon Karo syrup
½ teaspoon salt
1 cup brown sugar
½ cup buttermilk

(continued on next page)

School Sisters of Notre Dame
Celebrating **175** *years*

Mix ingredients in saucepan and boil till it forms soft ball in ½ cup cold water. Pour over warm cake. It will soak in.

Submitted in 1993 by Mary Catherine Dundon, SSND from Milwaukee, WI

 Money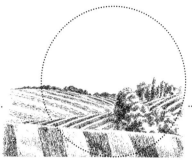

Searching out the lowest-priced food is not always the best way to be good stewards of our money.

Often it's the farmer, farmworker, and farming community paying the price for the low cost.

Buying local, seasonal foods (and fairly traded foods from far away when appropriate) benefits the farmer directly.

Simply in Season Study Guide
www.worldcommunitycookbook.org/season/studyguide.html

School Sisters of Notre Dame
Celebrating **175** *years*

Prune Whip and Custard Sauce *1925*

Serves 6

This recipe appeared in a cookbook put together by the 1901 class of the Academy of Our Lady (A.O.L.) in 1925 to raise money for the chapel.

¼ **pound prunes**
3 egg whites
⅓ **cup sugar**
1 teaspoon lemon juice

Pick over and wash prunes, soak overnight or several hours in water to cover. Cook in same water or steam in a strainer over hot water until soft. Drain off any surplus moisture. Remove stones and rub prunes through a strainer. Add sugar. Cool mixture. Beat the whites of eggs until stiff, add prune pulp gradually, and then add lemon juice. Pile lightly on a serving dish and serve with custard sauce.

323

Custard Sauce:
3 egg yolks
¼ **cup sugar**
⅛ **teaspoon salt**
1½ **cups milk**, scalded
½ **teaspoon vanilla**

Beat eggs slightly. Add sugar and salt. Stir constantly while gradually adding the hot milk. Cook in double boiler, stirring constantly, until mixture thickens and coats the spoon. Chill and flavor. If cooked too long sauce will curdle. Beating with a Dover egg beater will restore the smooth consistency.

Submitted by Mary Charissia Powers, SSND (deceased)

School Sisters of Notre Dame
Celebrating **175** *years*

Puffballs

Makes 50

½ cup (1 stick) butter or margarine
1 bag caramels
1 can condensed milk
2 bags marshmallows
Rice Krispies

Put butter, caramels and milk into a heavy saucepan and heat on low. Mix well until all caramels are melted. Keep on low heat. Drop each marshmallow into melted caramel mixture to coat, and then drop it into Rice Krispies. Toss around until well covered. Remove and put on wax papered cookie sheets. These freeze well.

324

Submitted by Rose Anthony Krebs, SSND from Mankato, MN

Pumpkin Pie Fudge

Serves 12-15

1½ **cups granulated sugar**
½ **cup pumpkin,** mashed
⅔ **cup evaporated milk**
2 **tablespoons margarine**
½ **teaspoon salt**
1½ **teaspoons pumpkin pie spice**
1 **package vanilla flavored baking chips**
2 **cups miniature marshmallows**
⅓ **cup nuts,** chopped
1¼ **teaspoons vanilla extract**

325

Lightly grease the sides and bottom of a medium saucepan.
Place sugar, pumpkin, evaporated milk, margarine, salt and
spice in saucepan. Stir constantly over medium heat. Boil for
12 minutes.

Remove from heat and add chips and marshmallows. Stir until
melted. Stir in nuts and vanilla. Pour into 8-inch square pan lined
with foil and greased. Chill until set. Cut into squares and enjoy.

Submitted by Mary Beck, SSND from Mount Calvary, WI

Pumpkin Crunch

Serves 15

1 (16-ounce) can solid pack pumpkin
1 (12-ounce) can evaporated milk
3 eggs
1½ cups sugar
4 teaspoons pumpkin pie spice
½ teaspoon salt
1 package yellow 2-layer cake mix
1 cup pecans, chopped
1 cup margarine, melted
Whipped topping

326

Preheat oven to 350 degrees. Grease bottom of 9X13 inch pan. In mixing bowl, combine pumpkin, milk, eggs, sugar, pumpkin pie spice, and salt in large bowl. Pour into pan. Sprinkle dry cake mix evenly over pumpkin mixture. Top with pecans. Drizzle melted margarine on top. Bake for 50-55 minutes or until golden brown. Cool completely. Serve with whipped topping. Refrigerate leftovers.

Submitted by André Aubuchon, SSND from St. Louis, MO

Pumpkin Pie Cake

Serves 20

*"Thanks for coming to 'my house.' I enjoyed the time together. Here
is the recipe for the Pumpkin Pie Cake." These words by the late Mary
Ann Fischer, SSND were emailed to our Extended Life Community after a
meeting. Mary Ann was appointed by Bishop Liebrecht in August 2002 to
be the second Parish Life Coordinator in the Diocese of Springfield-Cape
Girardeau, Missouri. Mary Ann died of lung cancer in September 2002.*

4 eggs, slightly beaten
1 (16 or 20 ounce) can pumpkin
1½ cups sugar
2 teaspoons pumpkin pie spice
1 teaspoon salt
1 (12-ounce) can evaporated milk
1 (18-ounce) box yellow cake mix
1 cup (2 sticks) butter or margarine, melted
1 cup pecans, chopped

327

Mix first six ingredients in order listed; pour into 9X13 inch pan.
Sprinkle cake mix over filling and pat down. Pour melted
margarine over top of cake, and sprinkle with pecans. Bake at
350 degrees for 1 to 1½ hours or until knife comes out clean when
inserted. Serve warm or chilled, plain or with whipped topping.

Submitted by Francine Koehler, SSND from Columbia, MO

School Sisters of Notre Dame
Celebrating **175** *years*

Rhubarb Custard Pie

Serves 8-10

2 eggs, beaten
2 tablespoons milk
1½ cups sugar
3 tablespoons flour
¼ teaspoon salt
¼ teaspoon nutmeg
3 cups rhubarb, chopped
1 tablespoon butter or margarine
9 inch pie shell, unbaked

328

Combine eggs, milk, sugar, flour, salt, nutmeg and mix with rhubarb. Pour into unbaked pie shell. Dot with butter or margarine. Bake at 450 degrees for 15 minutes, then 30 minutes more at 325 degrees until custard is firm and pastry is golden brown.

Submitted by Dolorita Sierszynski, SSND from Mount Calvary, WI

Rhubarb Torte

Serves 24

Crust:
1 cup butter or margarine, softened
2 cups flour
2 egg yolks
3 tablespoons sugar
1 teaspoon vanilla
¼ teaspoon salt

Mix together and pat into an oiled 9X12 inch pan.

Filling: 329
4 egg yolks
1 cup coffee cream
2 tablespoons butter or margarine
1½ cups sugar
4 tablespoons flour
4 cups rhubarb, chopped

In a mixing bowl, beat together the egg yolks and cream. Stir in the butter, sugar and flour. Add the rhubarb. Mix together and pour over crust. Bake at 375 degrees for 45 minutes.

Submitted by Rosemarie Dvorak, SSND from Red Lake Falls, MN

School Sisters of Notre Dame
Celebrating **175** *years*

Ricotta Cake

Serves 20

1 box butter recipe 2-layer cake mix
15 ounces ricotta cheese
3 eggs
¾ cup sugar
2 teaspoons vanilla

Prepare cake mix according to instructions on box. Pour batter into a greased and floured 9X13 inch pan. Set aside. Mix ricotta cheese, eggs, sugar and vanilla in a small bowl. Mix until well blended. Pour mixture over the cake batter until the entire area is covered. Bake at 375 degrees for 35-45 minutes. Cake is done when toothpick inserted in the center comes out clean. Cool and dust with powdered sugar before serving.

Submitted by Regis Krusniewski, SSND from Sarasota, FL

330

The myth that says EGGS ARE NOT HEART HEALTHY is just that, a myth.

EGGS enriched with omega-3 fatty acids are a useful source of the heart-healthy nutrient – but even with 200 milligrams of omega-3s, they contain only an eighth of the amount in a 4-ounce piece of salmon.

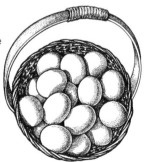

IF possible, use *ORGANIC EGGS from chickens that are given organic food, have access to the outdoors (cage free), and are free of antibiotics and hormones. There really is a difference in taste and quality.*

School Sisters of Notre Dame
Celebrating **175** *years*

Schaum Torte

Serves 16

This recipe appeared in a cookbook put together by the 1901 class of the Academy of Our Lady (A.O.L.) in 1925 to raise money for the chapel.

6 egg whites
2 cups sugar
1 tablespoon vinegar
1 teaspoon vanilla
Whipped cream

Beat the eggs to a stiff froth. Add the sugar gradually, then the vinegar and vanilla, beating all the time. Bake in two layers in a very slow oven, 275 degrees, one hour. Fill and cover with whipped cream. Serve whole on a platter with a spoon.

331

Submitted In 1925 by an SSND of A.O.L. in Chicago, IL

convent customs & traditions

I remember Schaum Tortes. They were in the shape of an "M" for a Marian feast day. Each sister had one at her plate in the motherhouse dining room. The big sugar cookies, a heart for Valentine's Day. How they delighted our hearts!"
Arlene Simon, SSND, MIlwaukee

School Sisters *of* Notre Dame
Celebrating **175** *years*

Sim Sim Pillow

Makes about 5 dozen

Sesame seeds are called sim sim in Kenya.

3 cups flour
1 cup sugar
1 cup shortening
4 teaspoons vanilla
1 tablespoon baking powder
3 eggs
½ cup sim sim (sesame seeds)

332

Measure into a bowl all the ingredients except the sim sim. Shape 2 teaspoons of dough at a time into 2-inch ovals. Roll the ovals into the sim sim. Place 1 inch apart on ungreased cookie sheets. Bake 15 minutes at 350 degrees.

Submitted by Mary Kerber, SSND in Nairobi, Kenya

Snowballs

Makes 3 dozen

1 cup peanut butter
1 tablespoon margarine
1 teaspoon vanilla
1 cup icing/powdered sugar
1 cup Rice Krispies
½ cup walnuts, chopped
Extra icing/powdered sugar (to make a thin icing)
Milk
Coconut

333

Cream together peanut butter, margarine and vanilla; mix in icing sugar, Rice Krispies and chopped walnuts. Put in fridge for a few hours to chill. Make a thin icing using the icing sugar and milk. Add the milk a little at a time until the desired consistency is reached. Remove the batter from the fridge, roll into tiny balls, dip into the thin icing and then roll in coconut.

Submitted by Joyce Lorentz, SSND from Regina, Saskatchewan, Canada

Sour Cream Raisin Pie

Serves 8 -10

1 egg
1 cup sour cream
1 teaspoon vinegar
¾ cup white sugar
2 tablespoons flour
¾ teaspoon cinnamon
½ teaspoon nutmeg
¼ teaspoon salt
2 cups seedless raisins
9 inch pie shell, unbaked

334

Beat egg lightly and blend in sour cream and vinegar. Combine sugar, flour, spices and salt and stir into first mixture. Add raisins and turn into unbaked pie shell. Bake in hot oven, 450 degrees for 10 minutes. Reduce heat to 350 degrees and bake 30 to 35 minutes more.

Submitted by Bernelle Taube, SSND from Northfield, MN

Special Cannoli Filling

Buy the cannoli shells in the Italian bakery.

4 pounds ricotta cheese
6 tablespoons regular sugar
½ cup citron, cut up very fine
2 drops vanilla
½ cup chocolate chips (small ones)

Work the sugar into the ricotta. Add other ingredients, mix and fill shells.

Submitted in 1992 by Filibert Spizzirri, SSND from Chicago, IL (deceased)

335

Fats Two GOOD FATS for your diet

Foods with *Omega-3 fatty acids*	Foods with *Monounsaturated fats*
Salmon	Canola & Safflower oils
Flaxseed	Almonds
Walnuts	Avocado
	Olive oil
	Natural Peanut Butter
	Olives

School Sisters of Notre Dame
Celebrating **175** *years*

Turtle Cake

Serves 15

1 box devils food 2-layer cake mix
14 ounces caramels
½ cup evaporated milk
½ cup pecans, chopped
1 cup chocolate chips

Make cake batter according to package directions. Pour ½ of the batter into a greased 9X13 inch pan and bake for 15 minutes at 350 degrees.

336

While cake is baking, melt caramels in a small pan with evaporated milk. Pour caramel mixture over hot cake batter. Sprinkle nuts and chips onto caramel. Pour on remaining cake batter. Bake at 350 degrees for 30 minutes longer. Moist and delicious.

Submitted by Sisters of St. Mary of the Pines, Chatawa, MS

Wackie Cake

Serves 10-16

1½ **cups flour**
1 **cup sugar**
3 **tablespoons cocoa**
¼ **teaspoon salt**
1 **teaspoon baking soda**
1 **teaspoon vanilla**
6 **tablespoons oil**
1 **tablespoon vinegar**
1 **cup water,** cold

Mix flour, sugar, cocoa, salt and baking soda and put in an oiled
8X8 inch pan. Make three holes. Put vanilla in one hole, oil in one
and vinegar in the last hole. Over this pour 1 cup of cold water.
Stir all together and bake at 350 degrees for about 40 minutes.

Submitted by Jacqueline Glessner, SSND, Hermanas de Nuestra Senora de
la Ensernenza from Lima, Peru

Whiskey Cake

Serves 16

1 (2-layer) yellow cake mix
1 (4-serving) box French vanilla instant pudding
4 eggs
1 cup milk
½ cup oil
1 shot glass (1½ ounces) of whiskey
1 cup chopped nuts
Flour

338

Pour all ingredients into mixing bowl except nuts and flour. Beat 5 minutes. Coat nuts in flour and fold into batter. Pour into greased and floured tube pan and bake at 350 degrees for 60 minutes.

Glaze:
¼ pound butter or margarine
1 cup sugar
½ cup whiskey

Melt (not boil) butter or margarine. Dissolve sugar and whiskey into margarine. Remove cake from oven. Poke holes into cake with a straw. While in pan, pour glaze over the cake. Let cake stand about an hour in pan.

Turn the cake out onto buttered waxed paper and then flip it immediately onto a plate.

Submitted in 1993 by Dorothy Malone, SSND from Cockeysville, MD

White Chocolate Covered Pretzels

Serves many

One package of vanilla chips
Pretzels or pretzel sticks

Melt vanilla chips. Dip in pretzels or pretzel sticks. Lift up with fork. Spread out on wax paper. Refrigerate or place on tray in freezer for a few minutes.

Submitted by Rita Mary Schweihs, SSND from Homer Glen, IL

339

Threeness

by Patricia A. Obremski, SSND

Water holds a secret
to her heart.
As ice, she joins her
interlocking circles to create
a universe of strength,
of beauty
stretching tiny pavement cracks,
flakes falling gently on a barren,
chilly landscape.
Melting, she baptizes,
sates thirsty roots, and
cleanses air made hazy
by the vagrant winds
of Earthly indiscretions.
Finally,
to rise as steam
with energy so awesome
powering engines to perform
unfathomed deeds.
With humble persistence,
she moves whole mountains,
then brews a cup of coffee
to soothe a drowsy soul.
A trinity of phases,
diverse yet one,
from unity of elemental bonds,
water proves herself
essential element of life.

GRACE
BLESSINGS &
RITUALS

As soon as they came ashore, they saw some bread and a charcoal fire with fish cooking on it.

Jesus said, "Come and have breakfast!" John 21: 9-12

Grace

over a thanksgiving meal

O God of seed and harvest, we pause to give thanks for the table set before us and the food that graces it.

(The people gathered take turns naming the various foods on the table being blessed, by saying, "thank you for the _____" until all the foods have been named.)

In a moment we will eat this food, harvested from many parts of the nation and world. It will be transformed into the flesh and blood of our bodies. Keep us mindful of the many workers who labor in field and factory to bring us this food.

May the nourishment of this meal strengthen us to work for justice and equity, in a compassionate and merciful way, among those who labor in the fields and workplaces to feed us. We pray this in the name of our Creator God, who not only fed the Israelites in the desert but calls and transforms each of us into disciples for justice and peace. Amen .

from Interfaith Worker Justice
http://www.iwj.org/

Grace at mealtime

✠

O Lord,

help us to remember where our bread comes from
and why we yearn for living waters.
Teach us your guiding principles of care for community
and reverence for Creation.
Show us how to turn the ground
into a sacred commons once again.

> Guide us to cover the earth with a new agriculture.
> Help us make a place at the table for everyone.
> Tell us that eating is a moral act.
> Then fill us with joy. Amen.

National Catholic Rural Life Ministry

344

---

*"Lord, to those who hunger,
give bread. And to those who
have bread, give the hunger
for justice."* Latin American prayer

Prayer for our meal

We call upon the waters that rim the earth,
> horizon to horizon,
That flow in our rivers and streams,
That fall upon our gardens and fields,
And we ask that these waters nourish us
> and all living creatures.
> Teach us and show us the way.

from a Chinook Blessings Litany

Grace before & after Meals from Janet Tanaka, SSND

O Lord, please bless this meal. May it become food for our heart as well as food for our body. Please give needed help to all those who are without food this day. Amen.

Lord, from our hearts we give you thanks for the grace of this meal. We who have shared this meal together are united in heart. May we always walk in your love. Amen.

Meditation before eating
by Thich Nhat Hanh and the monks and nuns of Plum Village, 2000

This food is the gift of the whole Universe– the Earth, the sky, and much hard work.
May we eat in mindfulness so as to be worthy to receive it.
May we transform our unskillful states of mind
and learn to eat with moderation.
May we take only foods that nourish us and prevent illness.
We accept this food to realize the path of understanding and love.

Grace remembering farm workers

"Giver of breath and bread,"
we give thanks for the food that graces our table and the labor of farm workers whose hands pick, lift, pack and carry the vegetables and fruits we enjoy. As this food nourishes our bodies, may our spirits receive the energy to seek with them the justice they so rightfully deserve. Amen.

from Harvest of Justice Table Prayers, 2002

The Cup of Our Lives

by Justine Nutz. SSND

Personal/Communal Variations of Cup Rituals

- Find a lovely cup. Bless it in your own way. Let its morning emptiness remind you to be careful of how you fill your day.

- Create a little dance or simple gestures using your cup.

- Spend prayer time slowly drinking a cup of water/coffee/tea... and considering the *seven liquids* (see page 347) of your life. How was each a part of the past year of your life?

- Community – put cups in a circle. As each of the *seven liquids* is read, drink from cup (tea, coffee, eggnog – whatever!) as a sign of acceptance. Share hopes for yourself – Church, family, community, world, planet – according to the feelings of each liquid. Consider how the liquids change at different times of life – some are on overload – some are absent. Sitting in a circle, sense the flow of the liquids through the group.

- Consider the cup as the whole planet, which holds all the liquids of all the creatures on/in it.

- Let us toast each other with the cups of our lives!
  Let us toast ourselves!
  Let God toast each of us!

What did Jesus have to say about cups?

The Seven Liquids of Our Lives

MILK...of my nourishings, friendships, hopes, comforts...

HONEY...of my joys, reconciliations, affirmations, healings...

BLOOD...of my courage, pain, passions, convictions...

SWEAT...of my labors, insecurities, fears, despairings...

TEARS...of my loneliness, betrayals, grievings, longings...

VENOM...of my hatreds, angers, jealousies, violence...

CHAMPAGNE...of my ecstasies, visions, delights, intimacies...

347

prosit (be well) – German

cheers – British

a votre santé (to your health) – French

l'chaim (to life) – Hebrew

alla tua salute (to your health) – Italian

sto lat (a hundred years) – Polish

Praying Your Food

by Justine Nutz, SSND

Learn a lesson from the way
the lilies grow...Matt. 6:27

Learn a lesson from the way
the carrots – apples – potatoes – onions grow...

Learn a lesson from the way
bread – cheese –honey – wine is made...

Learn a lesson from
the egg – the water – the chicken – the fish...

LOOK at the roundness of your plate/mandala
and allow it to focus you – center you –
pull you into the food/gifts upon it.
Say **GRACE** – choose something on
your plate/mandala or in your glass or cup.
Be present to it.
Pray to God with it – let it pray for you – let it pray in you –

348

Bread – Give me the blessing of everydayness
– of appreciation – the simple things.

Potatoes – Give me eyes that see in the dark –
help me be patient and wait for your hand
to lift me from the Earth's darkness.

Onions – Gently peel away my layers, my masks –
make me unafraid to weep.

Carrots – I want to grow deep down
into the center of myself where I find truth.

Milk – I need comfort and consolation –
I feel helpless as a newborn baby.

Water – I want to be as fluid and clear as water –
I feel as if I am drowning in grief sometimes.

Banana – I need to be softer and more vulnerable.

hicken – Hold me close under your wings as a mother hen holds her chicks.

sh - Help me to swim and breathe in an nfamiliar atmosphere.

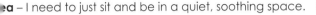

ea – I need to just sit and be in a quiet, soothing space.

ookies – Help me to savor the sweet and pleasant little moments.

lam/Oyster – I find it so hard to open up to some people.

> **Prune** – Hopefully, even as more wrinkles appear, more peace and serenity appear also.
>
> **Egg** – God of newness, be midwife to what has been growing quietly within.

avel With Your Food –   Go to Brazil with your coffee –
Colombia with your chocolate-
Central America with your pineapple –
California with your raisins –
the Orient with your rice –
Florida with your orange –
Eden with your apple –

349

ee your food in its first home –
;o to the sea. Climb a tree. Go into the earth. Walk through the fields.
ee the beehive. Hang on a tomato vine.

ee and thank the people involved in your food –
armers – fishermen – migrant workers – truckers – grocers – bakers

e aware of color – texture – shape – smell – taste. Think of memories
ssociated with some foods. Imagine foods going into your
loodstream to give you ENERGY, HEALING, VITALITY.
Vhich foods on your plate would Jesus have known?

EFLECT: At night – or whenever – perhaps something you ate that day ave you a bit of enlightenment – or made a connection – or helped ou be grateful – or broadened your global awareness – Write it down!

YOU ARE WHAT YOU EAT: Physically, emotionally, spiritually.

Happy Eating!

I believe that water . . .

I believe that water belongs to Earth and to all species.
I believe that water must be conserved for all time.
I believe that polluted water must be reclaimed.
I believe that water is best protected in natural watersheds.
I believe that water is a public trust to be guarded
   at all levels of government.
I believe that an adequate supply of clean water
   is a universal right.
I believe that water is life for the world.

Adapted from *"Water for Life! In Defence of our 'Sister Water'"* and
prepared by the ecology working group of the JPIC promoters, Rome, Italy 200
To see entire booklet go to: www.ofm-jpic.org/agu⊂

**After the 1992 Earth Summit,
the United Nations General Assembly
declared that March 22 of each year
would be recognized as
the World Day for Water.**

**Global water usage is divided
this way: agriculture 70%, industry 22%, and domestic 8%.**

**The UN Food and Agriculture Organization estimates that 100
tourists use the same amount of water in 55 days that could
grow rice to feed 100 local villagers for 15 years.**

EARTH & PEOPLE-FRIENDLY
FRIENDLY
HELPS and HINTS

Cleaners
Food Hints
Household Hints

Earth and People-friendly CLEANERS

As we become more aware of the damage chemicals are doing to our Earth, the way we clean and take care of our houses is also changing. Look under your kitchen and bathroom sinks, and you will probably find an array of disinfectants, polishes, stain removers, toilet, drain and oven cleaners that create damage in their production as well as in their use and disposal.

As we "buy into" the messages we receive from advertising, we find ourselves also "buying into" a mind set that instills a fear of germs and dirt, creating in us the desire to protect our families with the best products on the market. Unfortunately, many of these products are unnecessary, and some are downright harmful.

We invite you to step out of the cultural norm and create your own cleaners that address most household cleaning needs with **simple and safe ingredients: baking soda, white vinegar, borax, liquid soap and vegetable oil.** These ingredients are good for humans as well as the whole Earth community!

All-purpose cleaner

One quart warm water, one teaspoon liquid soap, one teaspoon borax and one teaspoon vinegar. This solution will clean most surfaces including countertops, floors, walls, tile, rugs and upholstery. Keep it in a spray bottle ready for use on small jobs.

Toilet bowl

For a thorough cleaning, empty the water in the bowl by pouring a bucket of water into it. Sprinkle baking soda on a wet rag, and scrub the bowl inside and out.

Tub, Sink,

Sprinkle baking soda on a wet rag and rub. Rinse well to avoid leaving a film. If a stronger cleaner is needed, use borax the same way. *(Borax can be purchased at a grocery store.)*

Glass

Use a spray bottle and solution of two tablespoons of vinegar to one quart of water. Wipe dry with old newspapers. Or spray the newspaper and then clean the glass.

Floors

For vinyl floors damp mop with a solution of two tablespoons of vinegar to one quart water. For wood floors, use two tablespoons vinegar per gallon of water.

Drains

Prevent problems by not letting grease or hair go down a drain. If a drain becomes clogged, use a plunger, or pour in one quarter cup baking soda followed by one-half cup vinegar, and let them fizz for a few minutes. Flush with boiling water.

Mold and mildew

Prevention is the best solution. Keep shower area dry by using the fan and by wiping moisture off the tile with a squeegee after every shower and bath. If mildew still appears, scrub with baking soda and borax.

Oven

Ease spill clean up by placing a metal tray under baking dishes. If that fails, sprinkle soda on spills when they are warm; scrub off when cool. Periodically clean surfaces with moistened baking soda and a nylon scouring pad.

Wood furniture

On unvarnished wood use a natural oil such as linseed or almond. Let soak into the wood for an hour or so and remove excess oil with a soft cloth. Varnished surfaces don't need oil. Clean with a damp cloth and rub dry.

Earth and People-friendly
FOOD HINTS

EGGS

ECO-FRIENDLY DYED EGGS Why not make your own homemade egg dye from spices, fruits, vegetables and tea? To make the dye, mix one tablespoon of spice, five tea bags or four cups of chosen fruits or vegetables. Next, add four cups of water and two tablespoons of vinegar. Bring mixture to a boil. Make as many colors as you choose and pour into separate bowls for dipping eggs.

- **Pinks and reds – frozen fruit such as raspberries and strawberries or beet juice.**
- **Orange – paprika**
- **Deep yellow – turmeric**
- **Light green – spinach**
- **Purplish/blue – blueberries, red cabbage or grape juice**
- **Brown – strong coffee or tea**
- **Orange – chili powder**

Keeping lemons fresh Lemons keep for weeks if you put them whole, into jars, cover with cold water and close tightly. They give more juice, too.

Keeping cookies crisp Put a piece of tissue paper in the tin with your cookies. To keep your cookies moist, put a piece of apple alongside.

Peel beets After boiling beets, dip them into cold water. The stems and skin slip off easily.

Perfect poached eggs Add one tablespoon white vinegar to the water. Swirl water into a whirlpool before dropping in eggs.

Tender corn-on-the-cob Adding a small amount of milk to the cooking water makes corn-on-the-cob sweet and tender.

Boiling potatoes When boiling potatoes, add mi
to the water. It improves the flavor and keeps th
potatoes white.

Rice and noodles Adding a small amount of canol
or olive oil to the water when cooking rice, noodle
or spaghetti keeps it from sticking together. Howeve
adding oil to the water when cooking spaghetti w
also make it more difficult for a sauce to stick to it.

Butter or margarine ?

The question, "Which is better, butter or margarine?" should be changed to, "Which is worse, butter or margarine?" Olive oil and liquid canola oil are preferred, since the solidifying process makes oils unhealthy. However, occasionally using

small amounts of real butter remains preferable to using any kind c
margarine.

The Big "Double OO"
OLIVE OIL

Olive oil is an excellent alternative to butter or margarine for use i
food preparation or for use as a condiment. It enhances the taste o
many foods and it has proven health ben-
efits. Because olive oil is so flavorful, less
is required to add flavor to food. This re-
duces the calories and the total fat content of food prepared or served with olive
oil compared to food prepared with other
less flavorful oils.

Olive oil contains a high percentage of monounsaturated fat, which
is healthier than the polyunsaturated fats found in corn oil and much
healthier than the saturated fats found in butter. Because olive oil i
vegetable based, it contains no cholesterol.

Earth and People-friendly
HOUSEHOLD HINTS

VINEGAR

Odor-eater

Vinegar is a great odor-eater. Put a little vinegar in a small glass or ceramic bowl and place it where you want to get rid of the odor. Rub vinegar on your hands to get rid of onion odor and stains from berries. Commercially made air fresheners and deodorizers are harmful to the environment and trigger allergic reactions in many people. They also cause harm in their production and disposal.

Removing scorch marks

To help remove light scorch marks on fabrics, rub lightly with undiluted white vinegar, then wipe with a clean cloth.

Pet urine on carpet

Clean up pet urine on your carpet by pouring undiluted white vinegar straight on the stain. Wipe clean with strong strokes and then blot with cold water. This cleans and deodorizes.

Removing coffee stains

After spilling your Fair Trade coffee, rinse area with cold water immediately. Rub a couple drops of a mild, white dish washing liquid and rinse well. Then treat with a mixture of one-part white household vinegar and three-parts water. Rinse again and launder as you normally do.

Candle wax

To get rid of candle wax from the tablecloth, let the wax harden. A quick way is to put it in the freezer. Then scrape it off the tablecloth with a dull knife. Set your iron on the warm setting. Place a paper bag on both sides of the stain and run the iron (no steam) over the stained area. Change the bag often to absorb all of the wax. Launder as usual.

Candle wax on carpet

Put ice cubes into a metal pan. Place it directly on top of the candle wax until it is frozen solid. With a small hammer, hit the wax to break it up. Pick up the pieces.

Ballpoint ink stain

Place the garment on a towel stain-side down. Lightly dampen a cloth with rubbing alcohol and gently dab *(do not rub)* the stain.

Carpet indents

Try applying moisture from a steam iron and then brush the nap of the carpet.

Steam iron

If your steam iron gets a little slack once in awhile, try running white vinegar through it. Let it steam until the  big bursts are over. After the iron has cooled, pour out the vinegar, then add water to the reservoir and rinse thoroughly. This should help it generate more steam.

Bar soap

Instead of tossing out the leftover sliver of bar soap, try pressing it firmly against a wet new bar of soap. Let it dry before using

Holiday hints

The best gift is the gift of yourself.

- Use newspapers or brown bags as wrapping paper. They can be appropriately decorated with recycled greeting cards.
- Sew scraps of cloth into drawstring bags as containers for gifts.
- Wrap a traveler's gift in old street or city maps.
- Visit locally owned stores with environmentally friendly gifts.
- Send electronic invitations and greetings and save paper.
- Be sure to set up an area to recycle wrapping paper at the gathering.
- Avoid using paper napkins, dishes, and cups as well as throwaway plastic utensils.

Model the behavior you would like to see, even when it means more work.

Getting rid of junk mail

• Write to DMA Mail Preference Service, PO Box 9008, Framingdale, NY 11735, asking to have your name removed from mailing lists. This is supposed to stop your name from being sold to large mailing list companies.

• If unwanted mail is accompanied by a return envelope marked "no postage necessary if mailed in the U.S. or Canada, etc.", fold up everything you have received and write a note next to your address label stating that you want to be removed from the mailing list and thanking them for recycling the returned paper.

• Cancel all the publications you don't have time to read and/or read magazines at the library instead of subscribing.

• If you are really serious and are short on time, join the Stop Junk Mail Association. For $17.50 they will do much of the work for you. Call 1-800-827-5549.

Plastic packaging

The best option is to avoid purchasing plastic packaging in the first place. Look for products in easily recyclable glass, metal and paper. When you have a choice, purchase a product in glass rather than plastic. Even when plastics get recycled, it's generally only once, whereas paper has many lives, and glass and metal can be recycled forever.

Grocery store bags

Put cloth bags in your car and bring them with you when you purchase food. Have the clerks use your own bags instead of theirs.

Education

WITH A GLOBAL VISION

For the past 175 years, sisters have adapted their ministries to meet the needs of their time and place.

Today School Sisters of Notre Dame educate wherever there is a need, always striving to empower women, to care for children and those who are impoverished, and to promote the integrity of creation, justice, and peace.

The ministries shown on the following pages express a special commitment to educating for intentional care of Earth.

Earth CENTERED MINISTRIES

School Sisters of Notre Dame,

educating for intentional care of Earth

reclaiming farming heritage,

bringing together land, food, charism.

Earth Spirituality Center 363

Mount Calvary, Wisconsin

Mary and Rose Beck, SSND

Located at Our Lady of Mount Carmel Convent in Mount Calvary, Wisconsin, the SSND founders of the Earth Spirituality Center are in the process of re-developing the land, bringing back together School Sisters and 40 acres of farm land and picturesque rolling hills formed by early glacial activity.

Founded by Mother Caroline Friess in July of 1852, the land was farmed by the Sisters and a hired caretaker until the 1950s when it was allowed to lie fallow. Recent awareness of the need to educate ourselves to a more intentional

(continued on next page)

care for the earth has ignited the hearts of SSND to reclaim our farming heritage.

Today participants in the Earth Spirituality Center's programs can help feed the pigs and chickens, collect eggs, harvest vegetables, prepare healthy garden meals, all the while learning about the cries of Mother Earth evoked by behaviors of human beings. Discovering how to align SSND spirituality within the broader context of Earth Spirituality is a transforming experience for those who attend weekend and weeklong Immersion Experiences at the Center.

Weaving together organic vegetable gardening, preparation of food, and care for the earth and animals with our SSND charism and ministries makes real our concern for the "integrity of creation."

For more information:

Earth Spirituality Center, Mt. Calvary, Wisconsin

Mary Beck, SSND
Organic Foods & Garden Director

Mary Ann Srnka, SSND
Director

Suzanne Moynihan, SSND
Education Director

110 Notre Dame Street
Mount Calvary, WI 53057
(920) 753-2131

$\mathcal{E}$arthrise $\mathcal{F}$arm
$\mathcal{M}$adison, $\mathcal{M}$innesota
Annette and Kay Fernholz, SSND

Earthrise Farm is a four-acre gift of land in the upper Minnesota River watershed in West central Minnesota directed by School Sisters of Notre Dame Kay and Annette Fernholz. Established in 1996, it is located on their 240-acre family farm where they live with and care for their parents.

Photo Patrick O'Leary

365

Through gatherings with a "rural life" community of other sisters from the order over the years, Annette and Kay began to seriously consider putting into practice the values they hold dear – caring for creation and restoring the environment. So 12 years ago they moved back to the farm and started their Center for Earth Spirituality and Rural Ministry. Its primary feature is a garden dedicated to community-supported agriculture (CSA). Shareholders from the area (and as far away as the Twin Cities) financially support the production of garden vegetables on the farm, and in turn receive a box of food each week for a 22-week season – enough to feed four people.

Earthrise also conducts programming for local schools, including a curriculum focused on sustainability.

True to the School Sisters of Notre Dame ministry of education, Earthrise also conducts programming for local schools, including a curriculum focused on sustainability. There are also classes at the farm on canning, bread-baking, pottery, and "Earth literacy." And Earthrise is a place where juveniles who are "sentenced to serve" by the county court system can come to do community service. "*Almost all of them say, 'I really like it out here,'*" notes Kay.

366

Honeycomb Center Peace is the newest addition to their well-rounded ministry. Located in an evergreen sanctuary, it is a circular Mongolian-like tent often referred to as a yurt. People wanting a place of rest can arrange a stay in the yurt, experiencing time in solitude and reflection.

Used with permission: University of Minnesota News, August 1, 2006. Article by Rick Moore.

For more information:

Earthrise Farm, Madison, Minnesota

Annette Fernholz, SSND
Kay Fernholz, SSND
Co-directors of Earthrise Farm

2580 250th St.
Madison, MN 56256
Office Phone: (320) 752-4700
http://earthrisefarmfoundation.org

Center for Earth Spirituality and Rural Ministry

Mankato, Minnesota

Since the inception of the Mankato Province of the School Sisters of Notre Dame atop Good Counsel Hill in Mankato, Minnesota, in 1912, until the end of the 1970s, the Sisters had among their ministries a working farm that supplied meat, dairy, eggs, grain, and produce for the sisters and students who lived there. Due to a variety of social and economic changes and the industrialization of agriculture in the U.S., this farm ministry was discontinued by the end of the 1970s.

EDUCATION & RESOURCE
Center

After the farm crisis in the 1980s, however, a renewed interest in small-scale, sustainable agriculture emerged, eventually leading to the founding of the Center for Earth Spirituality and Rural Ministry. The Center was founded in 1996 as a response to both the pressing concerns of rural people and the emerging environmental aware-ness of the sisters themselves.

Today the Center promotes and fosters awareness and ways of living that recognize and support the interconnection and interdependence of all life. One of the purposes of the Center is to model environmental stewardship on the SSND land itself through ecological awareness, ecosystem restoration, support of local food production, and environmentally sensitive maintenance practices.

In addition to an environmental education and resource center, the Center hosts a two-acre organic community garden that is tended by SSND sisters and staff, as well as immigrants, and low to moderate-income people from the area. Through retreats, discussion groups, community events, legislative advocacy and collaborative networking based on the social teachings of the Catholic Church and the Universe Story, the Center aims to recognize the sacred all around us.

For more information:

Center for Earth Spirituality and Rural Ministry, Mankato, Minnesota

Lisa A. Coons
170 Good Counsel Dr.
Mankato, MN 56001
(507)389-4272
lcoons@ssndmankato.org

Kathleen Mary Kiemen, SSND
St. Paul Site
561 Hamline Ave. S.
St. Paul, MN 55116
(651)690-2533
kkiemenssnd@yahoo.com

Orchard Sancta Maria in Ripa
Saint Louis, Missouri

The Sisters themselves did the farm work, providing healthy food for the community as well as some of the sisters on the missions.

369

Located on the banks of the Mississippi River in the mid-Mississippi River Valley, Sancta Maria in Ripa is the Motherhouse of the St. Louis Province. When it was established in 1895, the sisters lived on a fully sustainable farm. The land supported extensive vegetable gardens, an orchard of 100 fruit trees on four acres including apple, peach, pear, and plum trees, and a vineyard covering one acre. In addition there was a pasture for cows and a hennery for the chickens, ducks, and turkeys. The Sisters themselves did the farm work, providing healthy food for the motherhouse community as well as some of the sisters on the missions.

Today, a small orchard of fruit trees, apple, pear, plum and cherry still graces the land. No chemicals ever were or are now sprayed on the trees. Little brown spots on the fruit are not a deterrent either to the deer that forage the ground for fallen fruit, or the sisters who have enjoyed many a fruit pie, applesauce, pear butter, and jam.

Ripa Orchard

by Joyce Engle, SSND

In an earlier time
Sturdy young German women
Held the saplings in place—

Apple peach pear plum, berries over here—
And the rich Missouri soil welcome the roots.

These young women knew they too
Were transplants
Lining out an orchard for future hands.
Beyond what they could see,
The harvest would be for others.

370

And they did come-
Women of many backgrounds
Robed in black, with education on their minds
They walked amid the blossoming trees-
Their own roots trying the Missouri hillside.

As the fruit from those before them
Tumbled in dented cans
They pared with prayer and
Welcomed the abundant fruit
With youthful amazement.

Photo: Ray Flamm

They prayed their way through
Bushels of fruit;
Neither could their eyes see
How the seeds would be scattered.

Today, the remnant trees
Still brace the hillside-
Feel the plunder of deer and
The faithful harvesting of the caring few.

Still, sturdy roots penetrate Ripa's soil;
The flowering, we know, will surprise the future holde
As amazed as we have been at change's work.

All the works of God grow sturdier and sturdier,
And mysteriously,
Lovelier and lovelier.

Caroline Center

Baltimore, Maryland

Sponsored by the School Sisters of Notre Dame, Caroline Center was founded in 1996.

The mission of the center is to assist unemployed and underemployed women to acquire the discipline, knowledge, and skills necessary to find work in a career with potential for growth and advancement thus creating a future full of hope for themselves and their families. Now, in its 12th year, Caroline Center continues to fulfill this mission throughout the larger Baltimore metropolitan area.

One of the trainings that is provided is in the area of Culinary Arts.

371

CULINARY ARTS

For more information: Caroline Center, Baltimore, Maryland

Patricia McLaughlin, SSND
Executive Director
900 Somerset St.
Baltimore, MD 21202

410-563-1303
410-563-1302 (Fax)

www.caroline-center.org

Composting *in the Japan Region of the School Sisters of Notre Dame*

Because of the limited space in and around the city convents in Japan, the sisters of the Japan Region, along with many citizens in Japan and around the world, have been using the research of Dr. Teruo Higa for over 10 years to turn kitchen waste into some of the most effective fertilizer while cutting down on the amount of waste needing to be disposed of by local collectors. Dr. Higa is the Japanese scientist in Okinawa who began the research to find a natural solution to the imbalance humans are causing with waste treatment.

The process for creating fertilizer is quite simple and requires only a bucket with a spigot near the bottom and a dry EM "bokashi" mix.

372

Effective Microorganisms (EM) is the brand name of the product developed by Dr. Higa. The process for creating fertilizer is quite simple and requires only a bucket with a spigot near the bottom and a dry EM "bokashi" mix. EM "bokashi" is a dry mix of fermented organic material made from EM•1® Microbial Inoculant, molasses, water, and an organic (high carbon) material such as rice or wheat bran, sawdust, dried leaves, etc. The beneficial microorganisms in *bokashi* ferments food waste, preventing it from rotting.

As you prepare vegetables or fruits for a

meal (no meat products, please) collect all of the raw, dry peelings. Follow the directions on the bag of "bokashi" to create your own bucket of sweet smelling "garbage" that liquifies into collectable fertilizer that is so powerful you need to dilute it before using it in your garden for food or flowers. The garden at Iwakura Convent is a result of EM composting.

In Japan EM "bokashi" is readily sold in supermarkets. If you cannot find it in a market or garden center in your area, you can order it online by visiting the "web store" at www.emamerica.com. This site also gives a complete explanation of the EM process and other EM products.

If you are fortunate enough to have some space, time and personal energy available, you could organize a community collection center for your neighbors' "garbage" and convert your whole neighborhood to this more effective and natural form of composting.

373

André Maureen Soete, SSND

"Lunch Box"

In the Introduction to the delightful Centenary cook book we learn that it was "compiled at the request of our dear faithful House Sisters....Its purpose is to aid our busy Marthas in their loving labors to provide for the bodily needs and comforts of their Sister-companions."

Today, as we read these excerpts about preparing lunches, we are reminded that many of us tend to be "busy Marthas," grabbing lunch on the run, eating processed foods, or even fast food. Most of this food does not provide real nourishment for our bodily needs nor is it very comforting.

The gracious words of Sister M. Emma, SL, who wrote this so long ago, recall a less hurried age. Her words are an invitation to return to eating "slow food" – food carefully prepared with our total health in mind, food that is lovingly prepared, beautiful to look at, and nutritious as well. Today her words also remind us to consider the health of the Earth from which our food comes as we carefully choose what we put into our bodies.

– Excerpted from *Notre Dame Centenary Cook Book: 1847-1947*

"Lunch is a very important meal; therefore, it should not consist of a mere snack, but on the contrary, a lunch box should consist of a wholesome appetizing diet. In packing a lunch box keep in mind to make it nourishing and tasty and make sure there is plenty of it. It must carry well or it will not be appetizing when it is opened.

(continued on next page)

"Select a clean, large box and begin to select foods that give energy and contain vitamins. Citrus fruits and raw vegetables should abound...such things as carrots, parsley, tomatoes, radishes, cabbage, oranges, grapefruit, kumquats . . .

"In cold weather a hot dish may be prepared in the form of creamed soups or broths. In warmer weather cold fruit juices, milk or chocolate milk or eggnogs may be prepared. Some liquid form of food should be included to help digest the lunch . . . .

"A lunch box sandwich should be prepared with lettuce, pickles,

dressing, and the like to cheer up all sandwich lovers. Besides meat sandwiches there are other nutritious sandwiches that may be included as ground carrots, raisins, peanut butter; . . . . eggs, pickles, celery, dressing; . . . chopped prunes, cheese, nuts. Cut sandwiches in fourths or in a circular shape or any other that may please your fancy, top with a slice of olives, pickles, nuts, or other delicacies.

"Salads also play an important role in the lunch box. Some favored salads of this nature of our community are carrot, raisins, nut salad; cabbage, pineapple, nut salad; potato, olive salad; cabbage, raisin, orange salad; celery, cheese, nut salad.

"You may also include a cup containing relishes; such as, celery hearts, bud radishes, strips of carrots, pickles, or olives. Deviled eggs are pleasing to the eye. Fill small cellophane bags, which you have made in your spare moments with

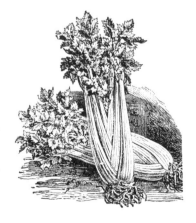

potato chips or cookies so they do not become soft. Nuts and

(continued on next page)

candies should be included for those who crave sweets. Canned or cooked fruits may be prepared in small jars for those whose diet does not permit fresh fruits. Never overcrowd the box with large fruits. Keep box well balanced. If no small fruits are available then dice the apples, cube or section oranges or grapefruits. **Fill all empty cracks so that the box will not be upset. This may be done by inserting pieces of candy, small bunches of grapes, whole stem cherries or vegetable flowers with sprig of parsley.**

"You will find that these lunch boxes are inexpensive and nourishing. Such lunch boxes are a source of surprise and delight to all travelers. A cheery personal note tucked in will prove to be the best after-dinner mint."

376

Index to Recipes

E

384

389

T

Twice-Baked Potatoes, 114

U
Upside Down Pizza, 204

V
Vegetable Salad, 67
Vegetable Soup for Winter, 36
Vegetarian Lasagna, 205
Virginia Pork Chops, 206

W
Wackie Cake, 337
Walla-Walla Treat, 115
Watergate Salad, 69
Water Lily Salad, 68
Whipped Sweet Potatoes in Orange Shells, 116
Whiskey Cake, 338
White Chocolate Covered Pretzels, 339
Wild Rice Casserole, 207
Winter Squash, 117

390

Y
Yeast Rolls / Bread, 268
Yummy Graham Wafer Cookies, 269
Yummy Summer Squash, 118

Z
Zucchini Rounds, 119
Zucchini Squares, 270

Acknowledgments

This book is the fruit of much collaboration among School Sisters of Notre Dame, their associates, staff, families and friends across time and space.

We are grateful to the School Sisters of Notre Dame (SSND) and their associates, within North America and beyond, who agreed to share some of their favourite recipes. We have also relied upon two previously published SSND cookbooks: the *Notre Dame Centenary Cook Book, 1847-1947* and the cookbook put together by the 1901 class of the Academy of Our Lady (AOL) in Chicago in 1925 to raise money for the chapel. Many recipes were also received from SSNDs around the world in the early 1990s when a cookbook marking the hundredth anniversary of the death of Mother Caroline in 1892 was proposed. Although that particular project did not proceed, the recipes have been included in this 175th anniversary project.

This project was initiated and overseen by the Development Directors of the North American Major Area of the School Sisters of Notre Dame: Ruth Emke, SSND, Pamela Giblon, Lynore Girmscheid, SSND, Mary Lewis, Linda Lynch, Irene Perez and Patricia Stortz. On behalf of the Development Directors, Linda and Pat formed the NAMA Cookbook Committee with Gen Cassani, SSND, Mary Eric Militzer, SSND, Rose Mercurio, SSND, Maxine Pohlman, SSND, Eileen Reilly, SSND and Paulette Zimmerman, SSND. This committee planned and brought the book to completion.

We thank the many sisters, associates, family and friends of SSND who graciously looked over and tested recipes. May God reward you for your generosity. If there are errors in this book, it is not for want of dedicated proof readers. Thanks go to Pat Murphy, SSND, Carol Stortz and Karla Mayer who gave hours of their time to this tedious task.

We are grateful to Murray Print Shop of Saint Louis, Missouri for their assistance in setting up the cookbook and in its use of environmentally friendly processes in the printing of it.

We are also grateful to the sisters, associates, friends and family who gave their support to this project in their kind words of encouragement and many prayers. May this work be a credit to your belief in the project.

Notes

Notes

Approximate Equivalents

Creating a cookbook that can successfully cross borders is a challenge. This is especially so when busy cooks rely on canned and packaged foods. Below are a few bits of information to make the conversion process easier. Note: cups are given in American measure. Imperial measure is slightly larger. For example: 1 imperial cup = 250 ml.

Can sizes *(approximate equivalents)*

oz	cups	ml	example
8	1	237	fruits, vegetables
10½ -12	1 ¼	284	condensed soups
12	1 ½	341	corn niblets
14	1 ¼	300	condensed milk
14 ½	1 $^2/_3$	385	evaporated milk
14 – 16	1 ¾	398	beans, cranberries
16 – 17	2	473	fruits, vegetables
20	2 ½	540	fruits, pie fillings
29	3 ½	796	vegetables

Approximate Equivalent Measures

Volume
1 tablespoon = 15 ml = ½ fluid ounce = 3 teaspoons
¼ cup = 60 ml = 2 fluid ounces = 4 tablespoons
$^1/_3$ cup = 80 ml = 2¾ fluid ounces
½ cup = 118 ml = 4 fluid ounces
1 cup = 237 ml = 8 fluid ounces
2 cups = 473 ml = 16 fluid ounces = 1 pint (American)
4 cups = 946 ml = 32 fluid ounces = 1 quart (American)

Dry measure: These vary according to the density of the ingredient.
1 cup butter/margarine = ½ pound = 237 g = 2 sticks
1 cup hard cheese (shredded) = ¼ pound = 114 g
1 cup all-purpose flour = ¼ pound = 114 g
1 cup chopped nut meats = ¼ pound = 114 g
1 cup chocolate chips = 6 ounces = 150 g

Oven temperatures

Fahrenheit	Centigrade
250	121
275	135
300	149
325	163
350	177
375	190
400	204
425	218
450	232